Culture, Language, and Society

Culture, Language, and Society

Ward H. Goodenough
University of Pennsylvania

The Benjamin/Cummings Publishing Company, Inc.
Menlo Park, California ● *Reading, Massachusetts*
London ● *Amsterdam* ● *Don Mills, Ontario* ● *Sydney*

This book is a
Benjamin/Cummings Paperback in Anthropology

Copyright © 1981 by the Benjamin/Cummings Publishing Company, Inc.
Philippines copyright 1981 by The Benjamin/Cummings Publishing Company, Inc.

Library of Congress Cataloging in Publication Data

Goodenough, Ward Hunt.
    Culture, language, and society.

    Bibliography: p. 121
    Includes index.
    1. Sociolinguistics. 2. Culture. I. Title.
P40.G64 1981   401'.9   80-20033
ISBN 0-8053-3340-1
ISBN 0-8053-3341-X (pbk.)
DEFGHIJKLMN-AL-8987

The Benjamin/Cummings Publishing Company, Inc.
2727 Sand Hill Road
Menlo Park, California 94025

Preface to the Second Edition

The first edition of this book was published in 1971 as an Addison-Wesley Module in Anthropology. In this edition, I have added a section on pidgin and creole languages to Chapter 3 and a corresponding discussion in the last part of Chapter 6. In Chapter 4, also, I have added a consideration of the view of culture formulated by Clifford Geertz. Other changes are minor.

My purpose remains the same: to clarify for students the nature of the phenomenon we anthropologists call "culture." That phenomenon, whatever its other characteristics may be, has content and organization. The nature of that content, what is involved in describing it, and its relation to society, the individual, and language comprise a set of interrelated matters crucial to the interpretation of human behavior, of human differences and similarities, and of human history. What we mean by culture, moreover, has long been and continues to be a subject of lively debate.

That I should take language as my point of departure for dealing with culture results from my exposure to the behavioral and social sciences as an undergraduate student when I took courses in personality theory and in cultural anthropology concurrently. In the one course, we concentrated on the processes in social interaction by which each individual acquires and maintains his or her particular conception or sense of self. We talked about "roles" and "role playing," but aside from this we had no model for what a conception of self consists of—no model of its content. We had no methods for describing any individual's conception of self, but characterized it in very general terms. In the anthropology course we talked about culture as something people learned and about cultural evolution and cultural borrowing and diffusion; but aside from some crude typologies, the best of which dealt with social organization, we had nothing resembling a working model of the content of culture. Descriptive ethnography had no developed methods (beyond what Bronislaw Malinowski suggested in consequence of his own intensive field experience) for describing how people in the societies anthropologists study perceive and understand what is happening in their world. It seemed to me at the time that developing systematic ways of investigating the content of self and the content of culture was the fundamental problem of the behavioral and social sciences.

In the following year, as a beginning graduate student, I had my first exposure to descriptive (structural) linguistics. I was impressed by the sophistication with which that discipline was handling the problem of describing content. Linguistics seemed in this regard to be by far the most advanced of the behavioral sciences. What linguists were learning about the nature of systems of speech behavior and the strategies they were developing for getting at the patterns in them—the content of language—seemed directly relevant to the problem of describing the content of patterned behavior generally. Others in my generation of graduate students found similar inspiration from linguistics for dealing with cultural description. In the thirty years since then, there has been much improvement in our understanding of the content of culture and in our ability to describe some parts of it with rigor. But there is a very long way yet to go.

So there is good reason for taking language as my point of departure to introduce students to the beginnings of what may someday be developed into a genuine model of the content of culture. At appropriate points I shall indicate the utility of our embryonic model for understanding culture change, but in this what I have to say can only be suggestive of directions for future thought and study.

Ward H. Goodenough

About the Author

Ward H. Goodenough is University Professor of Anthropology at the University of Pennsylvania. As an undergraduate at Cornell University, he majored in Scandinavian languages and literature. His Ph.D. in anthropology is from Yale. His field research has been in Papua New Guinea and in Truk and the Gilbert Islands in Micronesia. His published work has concentrated on social organization, the use of formal analytical methods in ethnography, culture change and community development, and Malayo-Polynesian languages. He is a member of the National Academy of Sciences, the American Philosophical Society, and the American Academy of Arts and Sciences.

Contents

Chapter 1

THE PROBLEM

The human tendency to see the world as divided into distinct peoples according to apparent, gross differences in language and custom seems to be nearly universal and to reflect something that is objectively real. The reality seems so obvious, indeed, that we take it as given and go on to consider the classic questions of anthropology regarding the history of languages and customs and the significance of the apparent differences among them, without stopping to examine critically the presumed reality.

People do, indeed, differ in language and custom. But the precise ways in which languages, cultures, and peoples relate to one another are more complicated than we commonly assume. Complications have been apparent to students of urban societies, which so often have populations of mixed ethnic and linguistic background, several social classes, many religious cults or sects, and highly specialized and differentiated occupations. Modern cities are often alleged, therefore, not be be amenable to description in the way anthropologists describe smaller, culturally more homogeneous communities. But the complications are not confined to modern cities. The South American Indians of the Northwest Amazon provide an illustration.[1]

---

[1] The account below is based on a report by Sorenson (1967).

In the heart of the Northwest Amazon Culture Area[2] is the Vaupes River. Together with its tributaries, it forms a drainage area about the size of New England, straddling the border between Colombia and Brazil. Aside from the numerically few Maku, the approximately 10,000 Indians living there are settled along the rivers, which are their highways for travel and transport. They all participate in a single network of intervisiting and intermarrying villages. And they all have similar customs relating to livelihood, housing and settlement, family and kinship organization, and religious ritual. But they speak more than 20 mutually unintelligible languages.

Each person is affiliated by patrilineal descent with a clan, whose adult males live together with their wives and children as a local longhouse group. A "tribe" consists of several clans that share a common name and are identifiable by their use of a distinct language. Thus the more than 20 languages are associated on a one-to-one basis with more than 20 tribes. Each tribe is also a political and ceremonial unit with a distinct history; and its several longhouses are located along a river several hours paddling distance apart. The tribes are linked in five named, exogamous phratries (brotherhoods). The rule of exogamy requires that husband and wife come from different tribes and consequently, from different language groups.

This arrangement requires that everyone know how to speak more than one language. In each longhouse the language of the tribe that owns it must be spoken in the presence of the men of the tribe. This is the primary language of the children born there. But the mothers of these children come from other tribes with other languages. The several in-married women from the same tribe speak their own tribal language when they are working or visiting together, but not when their husbands are present. There are frequent visits to and by a mother's kinsmen. Thus children are heavily exposed to their mother's as well as to their father's tribal language. Tukano, the language of the most populous and most widely spread tribe, serves as a *lingua franca* in the area and is also learned by children if it is not already either their father's or their mother's tribal language.

---

[2] The culture areas of South America are described by Steward and Faron (1959). For this area, see pp. 351-355.

The region, then, contains a population that is set off from other populations by conventions regarding marriage, exogamy, descent, long-house membership, and language usage (including use of a *lingua franca*). The population is subdivided into phratries, which serve mainly to regulate marriage. It is further subdivided into tribes, which are the largest ceremonial, political, and language-bearing units; and these are subdivided into clans, which are associated with local longhouse communities. At each level there are shared customs. At each level there is a sense of collective identity by contrast with other units. The contrast at the highest level is with the Maku, who live back from the rivers and marry among themselves, with other Indian groups that are located outside the region and have only sporadic contacts with its inhabitants, and with Europeans and mestizos (persons of mixed European and Indian ancestry).

What, then, are we to regard as a distinct people here? It seems clear that every level can be seen appropriately as a social and cultural isolate—a society or community of some kind. Every level has certain customs and conventions relating to some kind of subject matter. The usual uncritical equation of one language, one culture, and one people is unsuitable here. The relation of language, society, and culture to one another is clearly not a simple one in technologically undeveloped regions any more than it is in industrialized areas.

We shall begin our examination of this complex relationship with a consideration of language. Because of the special awareness of language that the art of writing gives us, and because of our experience with self-conscious efforts to learn second languages, we are able to look at language more objectively than we can look at most of the other kinds of conceptual-behavioral systems that make up the content of culture.

Chapter 2

THE CONTENT OF LANGUAGE

By a language we mean a body of standards for speech behavior, a body of organizing principles for giving order to such behavior. To learn French, for example, is to learn standards for communicative oral behavior and to develop skill in applying them both to shaping our own behavior and to apprehending the behavior of others (the others in this case being people we identify as speakers of French). A description of the French language is a description of the standards we need to know in order to speak in a manner Frenchmen will regard as acceptable French and to understand as well as they do what Frenchmen say to one another. To learn Russian is to learn another body of standards for communicative oral behavior.

There are, of course, several kinds of French, each with its own standards, and several kinds of Russian, a complication we shall consider later. The point still holds that a language, or particular dialect or version of a language, consists of standards.

The standards comprising every known human language may be seen as ordered into several systems or levels of organization: the phonological, morphological, syntactic, semantic, and symbolic. The last two involve the articulation of language with other aspects of culture and are often excluded from discussions of language as a distinct structural system, but it will be convenient to include them here in anticipation of our discussion of culture.

THE PHONOLOGICAL SYSTEM

The phonological system includes standards for discriminating the differences in sound, intonation, and stress that are consistently associated with differences in meaning. We hear the English words *tap, tab, dap* (as in fishing), and *dab* as all different, the voicing or nonvoicing of the kind of consonants technically called "stops" being a meaningful discrimination in English phonology (through voicing and nonvoicing have no meaning in themselves). A speaker of the language of Truk in the U.S. Trust Territory of the Pacific would be likely to hear these words as minor variants of the same thing, if he noticed any difference at all; for in his language the voicing and nonvoicing of stops produces no contrasts of meaning. On the other hand, native speakers of English have great difficulty perceiving the difference in Truk's language among the words *mwáán* ("male, man"), *mwmwáán* ("wrong"), and *mwmwán* ("fermented, soured"),[3] because in English we do not make meaningful distinctions according to the length of time a consonant or vowel is held, distinctions that are crucial in Trukese.

As these examples suggest, the phonological system of each language involves a set of discriminations by which speakers perceive what for that language are meaningful distinctions in sound. These discriminations are the **distinctive features** of the phonological system. They may be described in terms of the acoustical variables by which a hearer discriminates among them or, as is more usual among linguists, in terms of the behavioral (articulatory) variables involved in the production of distinguishable speech sounds: position of articulation, voicing, nasalization, spirantization, and so on for consonants; and tongue height, forward-backward tongue position, degree of lip rounding, and nasalization for vowels. Some variables—for example, position of articulation— serve to provide distinctive features in all languages,[4] but otherwise the

---

[3]The vowel *á* in Trukese has the quality of the *a* in English *hat*. The consonant written *mw* differs from plain *m* in that it is pronounced with the back of the tongue raised toward the back part of the roof of the mouth (where we articulate *k* in English). Double vowels are held for two syllabic beats (morae), and a double consonant is held for one syllabic beat, while single consonants have no syllabic duration.

[4]See, for example, the discussions by Hockett (1966) and Ferguson (1966).

particular distinctive features providing the basic discriminations for a language's phonological system appear to be a somewhat arbitrary selection from a wider range of possibilities. It makes very little practical difference, if any, whether a language is based on the sound distinctions of English, of Russian, of Japanese, or of any other known language.

For any particular language, then, there are combinations of distinctive features that are recognized by its speakers as making a difference in meaning. Such combinations as are needed to account for all meaning differences in a language are that language's **phonemes,** as they are technically called. Phonemes are the units of speech sound out of which a language's vocabulary is built. In the example we already considered, the sound units represented by the letters *t, d, p,* and *b* in the English words *tap, tab, dap,* and *dab* are phonemes of English but not of Trukese.

The standards making up a language's phonological system include principles for varying the pronunciation of phonemes according to the other phonemes with which they are juxtaposed. Thus initial /t/[5] in English (as in *tone*) are pronounced [tʻ] with aspiration (an accompanying puff of breath), but /t/ after /s/ (as in *stone*) is pronounced [t] without aspiration. We are ordinarily quite unaware of this consistent difference in our pronunciation of /t/ because it produces no meaningful contrasts in English. We need to refer to the distinction between aspiration and nonaspiration of consonants in order to describe the actual speech behavior of English speakers—the phonetics of English—but the distinction is not relevant for contrasting the meaningful sound categories, the phonemes, of English.

At a still higher level of organization, there are principles governing the sequences in which consonant and vowel phonemes may be arranged. Thus we can coin the words *plout* and *slout* in accord with

---

[5]It is customary to represent the symbols for phonemes between slash bars in order to distinguish them from symbols as used in ordinary writing, which often have only a partial correspondence with the actual phonemes of the language, as with the letters *c* and *k* in English orthography. Phonetic symbols indicating actual pronunciation are inclosed in brackets. Interested readers will find a good introductory account of phonology and the major articulatory dimensions in the texts by Gleason (1961) and L. R. Palmer (1978). For a fuller discussion, see Sommerstein (1977).

English standards of phonological order, but we reject *srout,* or *thlout,* or *ndout* as being contrary to those standards.

THE MORPHOLOGICAL SYSTEM

Built up from combinations of a language's phonemes are the minimal units that carry specific meanings in that language. These minimal meaningful units are technically called **morphs** (forms). For example, the English word *houses* contains two morphs: *house,* and the pluralizing suffix *-s* (phonemically /hawz-/ and /-iz/, the /s/ of /haws/ changing to /z/ with the plural suffix). Similarly, the Trukese word *semey* ("my father") contains two morphs: *seme-* ("father") and *-y* ("my"). The morphological system of a language comprises the various principles by which morphs are thus combined to form words, including the systematic ways in which their shapes are modified in these combinations, as with the change of /s/ to /z/ in the example of *house* above.

In describing a language, we consider the several variant shapes of morphs with the same meaning as different forms of the same thing. That same, abstract thing of which they are seen as different forms is technically called a **morpheme.** In English, for example, the pluralizing suffix written *-s* or *-es* has phonemically the several forms /-s/, /-z/, and /-iz/. Which one is used depends respectively on whether the morph to which it is suffixed ends in a voiceless consonant other than a sibilant, a voiced consonant (other than a sibilant) or a semivowel, or a silibant. Similarly in the Romónum dialect of Truk, the morphs of the morpheme meaning "district" appear with final vowels of different tongue height in compounds according to the height of the first vowel of the morphs suffixed to them, for example, *sópwu-tiw* ("lower district"), *sópwo-notow* ("western district"), *sópwó-tá* ("upper district").[6] There are a number of morphemes that follow this pattern of vowel alterna-

---

[6]Trukese has nine vowel phonemes: high front unrounded /i/, mid front unrounded /e/, low front unrounded /á/, high central unrounded /ú/, mid central unrounded /é/, low central unrounded /a/, high back rounded /u/, mid back rounded /o/, and low back rounded /ó/.

tion in which the final vowel of the first morph is always of the same vowel height (high, mid, low) as the first vowel of the suffix. Together they constitute one of the several classes of morphemes in the Romónum dialect, each class being characterized by its own distinctive pattern.[7]

THE SYNTACTIC SYSTEM

A language's syntactic system comprises its principles of **syntax**, the principles by which words are ordered into clauses and sentences. There are various functional categories (parts of speech) into which words and phrases sort themselves, and there are principles governing their sequential arrangement. Thus in Trukese a modifying word regularly follows the word whose meaning it modifies (*waa,* "canoe"; *waa seres,* "sailing canoe"), and a possessive construction linking two nouns regularly involves suffixing *-n* to the word for the object possessed and following it with the word denoting the possessor (*wáá-n Peeter,* "Peter's canoe"). When a modifying word is used in a possessive construction, it comes after the word denoting the possessor (*wáá-n Peeter seres,* "Peter's sailing canoe").

Syntax also involves the principles by which to transform one type of construction or sentence into another, as when we transform an active sentence into a passive one in English.[8]

THE SEMANTIC SYSTEM

The semantic system has to do with the standards by which people select particular words and expressions to convey particular meanings. In referring to a burning building, for example, one needs to know the criteria for deciding whether *house* or *barn* or *shed* is the suitable word. Similarly, when referring to someone's kinsman, one needs to know the criteria by which to decide whether he should be referred to as his *cousin,* his *uncle,* his *nephew,* or his *brother-in-law.* Here we become

---

[7] For a good introduction to morphology, see Gleason (1961).

[8] Linguists have developed several different approaches to syntactic analysis, one currently in vogue being that developed by Chomsky (1957, 1965). See also F. Palmer (1971) and L. R. Palmer (1978).

concerned with the standards by which people categorize phonemena of all kinds (things, events, relations, sensations, persons, personalities, etc.) and how they represent these categories by morphemes in their language and by expressions built from these morphemes. Thus the semantic system has to do with the way in which nonlinguistic forms—the entire range of concepts and percepts by which people apprehend their world—are mapped into linguistic forms, the linguistic forms serving as a code for the nonlinguistic forms. The nonlinguistic forms belong to the other conceptual-behavioral domains that comprise a culture; and the semantic system pertains to the denotative relation of the oral communicative domain we call language to these other domains.[9]

THE SYMBOLIC SYSTEM

The symbolic system comprises the principles governing the expressive and evocative uses of linguistic forms. *That's my father* and *that's my pop* denote the same kin relationship but express quite different attitudes of the speaker toward it. What is involved here is not so much the denotations as the connotations of words, not what they refer to but what they (or the things they denote, or they and the things they denote together) suggest or imply. There are associations of speech sounds with other kinds of sounds, for example, the sound of water. Speech sounds are also associated with various feeling states, such as disgust. There are the associations in experience that people have with the things particular words denote, as when we speak of *hearth and home.* Feelings of respect and disdain are associated with the use of particular words. And so on and on. The symbolic system is really a number of different systems having to do with nondenotative linkages of oral communicative behavior with other conceptual-behavioral systems. It also has to do with the way these linkages are systematically manipulated in speech to express feelings and evoke feelings in others,

---

[9] Analysis and description of semantic systems is much less developed than analysis of phonological, morphological, and syntactic systems. A review of semantics is provided by Leach (1974) and a discussion of problems and approaches can be found in Hammel (1965). Berlin, Breedlove, and Raven (1974) have produced a major monograph illustrating the semantics of Tzeltal botanical vocabulary.

to flatter and to insult, to build images, and to create moods.

Linguistic forms derive much of their shared (as distinct from idiosyncratic) symbolic value by virtue of social expectations or rules governing appropriate usage. Utterances may be grammatically acceptable and semantically meaningful and yet be regarded as inappropriate or as appropriate only under restricted conditions. The empirical study of how extralinguistic and extrasemantic considerations relate to language use has been aptly termed "the ethnography of speaking" by Hymes (1962).[10]

MEANING AS A PART OF LANGUAGE

Because analysis of the semantic and symbolic systems requires description of conceptual-behavioral domains other than that of oral communicative behavior, some linguists have taken the position that these systems are not a part of language or, at least, not a part of what is amenable to rigorous study by linguistic science alone. Some have argued that the analysis and description of a language should start with the phonological system. The morphological system can then be analyzed and described in terms of the phonological system, the latter being formally primitive to the morphological system; and the syntactic system can then be described in terms of the morphological, or in terms of the morphological and phonological taken together. Considerations of meaning are not only irrelevant but, for scientific rigor, taboo. Until recently, therefore, most scientifically oriented linguists have confined their attention to accounts of phonological, morphological, and syntactic systems; and they have left the compilation of dictionaries to more humanistically or more practically oriented students of language. This approach has been demonstrated to be overly rigid. Syntax cannot in practice be handled without reference to meaning, and phonology cannot always be satisfactorily described without regard to morphology, syntax, or even symbolic considerations, as when phonological distinctions convey no difference in semantic meaning but show whether or not the speaker is exhibiting respect to the person addressed. Several

---

[10] For examples of studies of this kind, see Bauman and Scherzer (1974).

less rigid and more productive approaches are now gaining favor. There is renewed interest in the methodological and theoretical issues of lexicography or dictionary making (Householder and Saporta, 1962) and in the way speech forms at the phonological, morphological, and syntactic levels convey symbolic as well as semantic meaning in social interaction (Hymes, 1962; Bauman and Scherzer, 1974).

There is, in this regard, a pertinent story about the great American linguist and anthropologist Edward Sapir, who had allegedly been working with an informant on an American Indian language with a grammar that he was having trouble sorting out. Finally, he felt he had caught on to the principles involved, and to test his hypotheses he began making up sentences in the language himself. "Can you say this?" he would ask his informant and would then produce his utterance in the informant's language. He repeated this several times, each time composing a different expression. Each time his informant nodded his head and said "Yes, you can say that." Here apparently was confirmation that he was on the right track. Then an awful suspicion crossed Sapir's mind. Once more he asked "Can you say this?" and once more received the answer "Yes." Then he asked, "What does it mean?" "Not a darn thing!" came the reply.

True or not, the story reminds us that it is one thing to be able to construct utterances that are phonologically and grammatically acceptable. It is something else to be able to communicate meaningfully. *Slow houses write stones* is grammatically correct English—in a narrow sense of the term grammar—but it is nonsense. In a wider sense of the term, it is ungrammatical to juxtapose as adjective and noun, subject and verb, and verb and object the particular semantic classes to which the words in that sentence belong. If the English language is what a person has to know in order to communicate meaningfully with speakers of English in a manner they accept as not significantly different from their own, then the semantic and symbolic systems are a part of what has to be known.

The systems comprising a language, then, are not only those that can be described in a sequential chain of formal development out of the phonological system. There are several different systems that are equally primitive to the whole, the whole being characterized by the ways in which these systems come together.

MULTIPLICITY OF PATTERNING

The linguist Charles Hockett (1966) has said that all human languages are characterized, among other things, by "duality of patterning." He had in mind that every language has both a phonological and a grammatical system. This duality of organization, he said, permits a large number of morphemes to be mapped into (represented by) different arrangements of a small number of phonemes. By learning to make a few phonological discriminations, people are able to process a very large number of information-laden messages. Hockett did not include the semantic and symbolic systems in his discussion. When we add these into consideration, it is evident that we are dealing not simply with a duality of patterning but with a multiplicity of patterning.

By this multiplicity of patterning, an infinite variety of experience can be mapped into a very large but finite set of concepts, which can be mapped into the different possible arrangements of an even more limited but still large vocabulary. The vocabulary consists of various arrangements of morphemes, which are composed of various arrangements of phonemes, distinguished from one another by different combinations of distinctive features (acoustical percepts).

We recreate these morphological elements by combining the limited number of phonological elements according to certain principles. We similarly recreate concepts by combining morphological elements into words and phrases according to certain principles. We recreate the complicated arrangements of these concepts that reflect life situations by combining words and phrases into sentences and the sentences into descriptive accounts and narratives, according to our principles of syntax and narrative construction. In this, we also evoke the subjective states that people have come to associate with these life situations. Thus, through language, we recreate experience; and by our ability to recreate it, we are also empowered to create all kinds of new, imaginary experiences.

Multiplicity of patterning is what makes language a powerful and efficient tool for objectifying and manipulating experience in what we call rational thought and for imagining a myriad of other things that we have never directly experienced at all. Without it, very little that we think of as human culture would be possible.

CLICHÉS

As powerful a resource as a language is for communicating experience with a high degree of subtlety, using it to express one's thoughts with precision is not always easy. Much of what we have to talk about in the course of everyday affairs, however, does not require great precision of communication. Stock words and phrases can be used over and over again. Once fabricated, expressions that effectively convey attitudes and feelings are likely to be used again when there is a similar attitude or feeling to be expressed. Most of what is said in ordinary conversation, therefore, is not made of words individually selected out of the speaker's vocabulary and fitted into a sentence one by one according to his principles of syntax. It consists largely of prefabricated sentences and phrases. "Hey, look at this!" "What do you think of that?" "Grin and bear it." These are items in a well-stocked storehouse of ready-made expressions that make up the clichés of English.

Clichés enable people to get on with the business at hand without having to wait for the stumblings and gropings that usually accompany efforts at originality in communication. The speaker does not have to figure out how to use his language to get where he wants to go. The clichés provide well-traveled pathways that he and his hearers already know well.

A language, then, is a far greater resource than is ordinarily used. Cultivating that resource, as we recognize in creative writing, is no mean art.

EMICS AND ETICS

Before we leave the content of language, there is an important conceptual distinction for us to consider, one that was first clearly formulated by linguists but that is fundamental to all behavioral science and crucial for cultural theory. This conceptual distinction is represented by the pair of terms **etics** and **emics**, coined by Kenneth Pike (1954) to represent for behavioral science in general the distinction in phonology represented by the pair of terms phonetics and phonemics. To see what is involved here, we turn back to our discussion of the phonological and morphological systems.

Recall the largely hierarchical relationship of words, morphs, phonemes, and distinctive features. The structure of words can be described in terms of their constituent morphemes and the rules governing the shape of a morpheme's several possible morphs, as we saw with Trukese words. The shapes a morpheme can take in its several morphs can be described in terms of rules governing the juxtaposition of phonemes, as we also saw illustrated in Trukese. The different shapes of the phonemes can be described as resulting from different combinations of distinctive features, the distinctive features being the percepts by which each phoneme is distinguished from all the others. To this point each level of organization could be described in terms of units within the language at a lower level of organization. But the distinctive features cannot be described with reference to other units within the language. To describe them, we must resort to concepts relating to the acoustics of speech sound or to what happens in the mouth when sounds are produced. We describe them in terms of such things as aspiration, nasalization, and position of articulation. These variables are not a part of the Trukese language or of the English language. They belong to a kit of concepts with which linguists try to describe any and all sounds that can play a role in language somewhere. When we speak of this kit or of its use in description, we speak of phonetics.

When a linguist starts out to record a language he does not know, he uses a phonetic notation system, one that takes account of all the variables that go into the production of speech sounds and with which he can record all the sounds he thinks he hears with detailed precision. Some of the distinctions in his transcription reflect distinctions that are meaningful for speakers of that language. Others may reflect consistent habits of speech that require description but that do not make a meaningful difference, such as the regular difference among English speakers between the pronunciation of /t/ in *tone* and that of the same phoneme in *stone*.[11] Many others reflect nothing that is either consistent or mean-

---

[11] It is characteristic of the speech habits of most American speakers of English that voiceless stops are pronounced with aspiration when they initiate a stressed syllable, unless they are immediately preceded by an /s/ in the same word; in the latter case they are unaspirated. Compare the *k* in *kin* and *skin*, the *p* in *pine* and *spine*, and the *t* in *internal* and *hysterical*.

ingful in the habits of the people whose speech is being recorded. An object of analysis is to sort out all of these irrelevancies. What makes it tricky is that variations in sound that are irrelevant in one language may be significant in another. As his analysis progresses, the linguist reduces the number of symbols with which he transcribes the language to the minimum number needed to represent the categories of sound that speakers of the language must discriminate, that is, the language's phonemes. Where a phonetic transcription seeks to represent everything that is distinctive in actual speech behavior, significant or not, a phonemic transcription seeks to represent only what is significant for the particular language in question.

The phonetic transcription represents a set of concepts by which linguists describe speech sounds. A phonemic transcription represents the sound categories that make a meaningful difference in some one language, and which provide the most appropriate points of reference for describing the phonological structure of morphemes and words in that language.

Generalizing from this, we may say that when we describe any socially meaningful behavioral system, the description is an emic one to the extent that it is based on elements that are already components of that system; and the description is an etic one to the extent that it is based on conceptual elements that are not components of that system. The object of emic analysis is to arrive at a minimal set of conceptual components that can serve as the primitive points of reference for describing the rest of the content of the system. But this minimal set of conceptual components can only be described in etic terms, that is, with reference to concepts that are extrinsic to the system being described.

Emics, then, refers to all that is involved methodologically and theoretically in making emic descriptions of socially meaningful behavioral systems, both linguistic and cultural. Etics refers to all that is involved in conceptualizing and describing the basic or primitive emic components of such behavioral systems. Moreover, because etic concepts are intended to be capable of describing the primitive emic components of any behavioral system of a particular type (for example, of systems pertaining to phonology, music, colors, physical shapes, genealogical relationships, logical relationships, and so on), they provide the frame of reference, the conceptual constants, through which to examine the similarities and differences among specific behavioral systems of that type. Thus, we use etic concepts when we compare Trukese with European music or make a comparative study of how people categorize kin relationships.[12]

There are relatively few subject matters for which we have well-developed bodies of etic concepts capable of describing the basic emic components of the behavioral systems pertaining to these subject matters. Speech sounds (phonology) happen to be one such subject matter. Genealogical kinship is another. The etics of some aspects of technology is also well developed, as revealed by the technical vocabularies for knot tying, plaiting and weaving, and pottery making; and important pioneering efforts have been made by Birdwhistell (1953, 1970) to develop an etic notation for communicative body movements and gestures. But the continuing undeveloped state of etics in the social and behavioral sciences results from inattention to emic descriptions of most behavioral systems in alien cultures. The development of phonetics is instructive in this regard.

When Europeans first began to describe exotic languages, they used the categories of sound of their own languages, as represented in their own alphabets, to record and describe what they thought they heard. And they used the categories of Latin grammar to describe the grammars of these languages. The result was most confusing, and observers

---

[12]The roles of etics and emics in description and comparison in cultural anthropology are discussed by W. Goodenough (1970, pp. 104-130). A now classic account of emic categories in a system of color classification is that by Conklin (1955). For an exploratory exercise in an emic account of some aspects of a folk religion, see Frake (1964); for the emic approach's usefulness in clarifying a long-held misunderstanding of African "ancestor cults," see Kopytoff (1971). See also the emic account of the Navajo classification of objects at rest by Witherspoon (1971). Some linguists, following Chomsky and Halle (1968), have recently abandoned phonemes in favor of a higher (they call it "deeper") level of abstraction, sometimes referred to as the morphophonemic level, in which what were phonemes and their distinctive allophones are treated together as phonic expressions of morphophonemes ("deep structure"), with rules for how to get from the alphabetic symbols representing the morphophonemes to the actual phonic representations in speech behavior ("surface structure"). (See Sommerstein, 1977.)

often decided that these languages lacked the degree of phonological and grammatical order to be found in European languages.

Progress was made as linguists paid attention to the things they had to learn to distinguish in order to get at the phonemes of other languages. They found that in some languages, for example, there are meaningful distinctions based on whether or not two vowels are separated by a break in sound made by closure of the glottis. Glottal closure was therefore added to the kit of concepts that might be useful in describing the meaningful distinctions of sound in other languages. Aspiration of consonants, meaningful in Hindi, was similarly added. The kit of possibilities expanded in this way, until linguists found no meaningful distinctions being made in new languages that could not be described in terms of the phonological variables they had already learned to take account of in the languages they had described earlier. The various distinctions they had learned to make by attention to the emics of languages could now be reexamined and their relations to one another explored. The result is modern articulatory phonetics—a systematized body of conceptual variables by which we can take account of all distinctions in speech sounds needed to describe the speech habits of the speakers of any known language (Pike, 1943; Hockett, 1955; Smalley, 1968). Because these concepts are universally applicable (though not universally relevant), we can make controlled comparisons of the phonological systems of different languages.

Such will become increasingly possible for other behavioral systems as we seek to make emic descriptions of large numbers of them, descriptions that try to account for everything that makes a significant difference within each system. In this way, the etics of socially meaningful behavior of all kinds will eventually be developed, and the study of other aspects of culture will achieve the rigor that we now associate with the study of languages.

Chapter 3

LANGUAGE, INDIVIDUAL, AND SOCIETY

LANGUAGE, DIALECT, AND IDIOLECT

We think of a language (or dialect) as being a single unitary system of standards, but we should not let this blind us to the considerable autonomy of the systems or subsystems within a language. Change in one may precipitate change in another, but each system is capable of considerable variation independent of variation in any other. The same phonemes can be combined according to different principles into two sets of structurally quite dissimilar morphs. The principle of vowel harmonics mentioned earlier in connection with the morphology of Trukese words can apply equally well to any phonological system whose vowel phonemes are distinguished, among other things, according to tongue height. The same concepts and percepts can be mapped into morphologically quite different vocabularies; and conversely, morphs of identical shape can denote different concepts and percepts (as with the noun and verb both spelled *egg* in English). This autonomy of the several systems within a language helps give to every language its quality of arbitrariness.

A language or dialect, then, is composed of a number of systems of varying degrees of autonomy, these systems being articulated in a particular way. Change in any one of these systems or change in the manner of their articulation will result in a somewhat different language. No two speakers of what we usually regard as the "same" language actually operate with identical systems and articulation of systems. Each speaker has his own **idiolect,** a term that has been used in somewhat different senses by different authorities but that here means the individual's own version of what he perceives to be a particular dialect or language. If this is so, what then are we to mean by a language, as when we speak of the English or the French language?

What we mean by a language in this sense is a range of variance among idiolects that does not impede too severely the several speakers' ability to communicate with one another effectively enough for ordinary day-to-day purposes. Noticeable differences within this variance are the basis for distinguishing **dialects.** When the variance among individual speakers is sufficiently slight as to go very largely unnoticed by them, they speak the "same" dialect.

Two dialects that are mutually unintelligible are dialects of two distinct **languages,** taxonomically speaking. Take a dialect of French, such as Francien (spoken around Paris), and a dialect of German, such as Swabian, for example. There is no question that they belong to distinct languages. But it sometimes happens that in a set of dialects A, B, and C, dialect B is mutually intelligible with dialects A and C, but A and C are not mutually intelligible with each other. If dialect B became extinct, we would say that dialects A and C are different languages and not dialects of the same language. When this situation occurs in which there is a chain of mutual intelligibility among a number of dialects but the dialects at the extremes of the chain are not mutually intelligible, for some purposes we may speak of all of them together as dialects of one language, while for other purposes we may speak of the extreme dialects as different languages.

What we have been talking about closely parallels the biological concepts of species and subspecies. No two individuals within a population are phenotypically or genotypically identical (unless they are identical twins, in which case they are genotypically identical). So long as the differences among individuals do not interfere with their mating with one another and also permit the production of viable offspring when they do mate with one another, we say that the individuals are members of the same species. Regional populations that are noticeably different in their prevailing phenotypic characteristics are subspecies of the same species, if individuals from the two populations at adjoining boundaries of their respective regions mate with one another and produce viable offspring. There are chains of animal populations such that A interbreeds with B, B with C, and C with D, but A and D, although overlapping in their territories, do not interbreed, behaving as distinct species (Mayr, 1963, pp. 507-512).

The criteria that define a language and a species—the ability to communicate in the former case, and the ability to mate reproductively in the latter—work in similar ways and pose similar problems. We should not dismiss the similarity on the grounds that biologically an individual can have only one phenotype, whereas linguistically he may be bilingual or multilingual, for then we would confuse individuals with systems. The ability to mate productively happens to depend very largely on factors that are determined by genetic systems. When we talk of a species, we refer to the capacity of individually inherited genetic systems to interact in a biologically productive way through the mating behavior of individuals. The ability to communicate effectively depends on factors that are determined by learned sign-symbol systems. When we talk of a language, we refer to the capacity of individually learned sign-symbol systems to interact in an intentionally productive (purpose-accomplishing) way through the speech behavior of individuals. What we are classing together as one species or subspecies are not really individuals—although we usually think of them that way—but different genetic systems carried by individuals. Similarly, and more obviously, what we classify together as one language or dialect are different idiolects, sign-symbol systems, carried by individuals. The processes or mechanisms by which individuals come to carry genetic and sign-symbol systems are very different, to be sure, but that is beside the point.

LANGUAGE VARIANCE AND MUTUAL INTELLIGIBILITY

Since idiolects and dialects may differ somewhat independently in any of their constituent systems or subsystems and also in the ways these systems articulate with one another, it behooves us to ask which kind of difference is more likely to be productive of mutual misunderstanding or mutual unintelligibility: difference within any one system or difference in the articulation of two systems with each other. Offhand, we expect that difference in the articulation of two systems—say the phonological and the morphological, or the morphological and the semantic—will be more quickly productive of misunderstanding than will difference within any one system itself. This judgment seems reasonable, also, in light of what we know about systems in general. Variation within any subsystem has less effect on the larger system of which it is a part than does variation in the way the several subsystems articulate with one another; for the structure of the larger system is most immediately characterized by the pattern of subsystem articulation.

Given little difference in the other systems, two speakers can differ considerably in their phonological systems without seriously impairing their ability to understand one another. We may have to take a little time to get used to one another, but most of us have little difficulty understanding people who speak our language with quite thick foreign accents. People learning a second language tend to use the distinctive features of their first language as a basis for distinguishing and pronouncing the phonemes of the second. Consequently they miss some phoneme distinctions entirely, just as a native German speaker tends, when speaking English, to fuse the phonemes /ð/ (voiced *th*) with /d/ and /þ/ (voiceless *th*) with /t/.

Some differences in morphological systems can also have little effect on mutual intelligibility. The rules governing the height of final vowels in compound words illustrated earlier for the Romónum dialect of Truk vary considerably among Truk's several dialects. The same nine vowel phonemes (see footnote 6) appear in all of these dialects, but the rules of vowel harmonics differ from one to the next, so that we find *sópwó-tiw* ("lower district") as well as *sópwu-tiw*, and *sópwo-wu* ("outer district") and *sapwo-wu* as well as *sópwu-wu* or *sópwu-u*.

Misunderstanding is bound to develop rapidly, however, with differences in the semantic system, that is, with the way concepts are mapped into morphs, words, and other expressions. By assigning to ordinary words in the Trukese language a set of different denotations, members of a traditional group of political specialists in Truk are able to speak in public and convey messages to one another that are not understood by the uninitiated. Thus the Trukese word *aaw* ordinarily denotes the large tree *Ficus carolinensis,* but in this special argot it denotes the son of a chief, ordinarily referred to by another expression. Speakers of this argot use Trukese phonology, mórphology, and syntax with only minor alterations, but by assigning special meanings to the words they use, they make themselves unintelligible to other speakers of Trukese. By the criterion of mutual intelligibility, they speak a different language.

When we think of learning a new language, although we recognize that it may involve learning some new rules of grammar, most of us think of the task as primarily one of learning a new vocabulary to represent the same old things. What we call a *house* in English is called *maison* in French and *iimw* in Trukese. We may later discover that the class of phenomena designated by *house* is not identical with the classes of phenomena designated by *maison* or *iimw* and that thinking in French or Trukese involves in each case somewhat different percepts and concepts than does thinking in English. But even if this were not the case, if French and English had the same phonology, the same patterns of morphological construction, and the same principles of syntax, and if the words in one language denoted the same things that the words in the other did, if at the same time the shapes of the words in the two were always different, the same shapes never designating the same things, we would regard them as different languages.[13]

The matter of variance boils down to this, then: so long as we can recognize in the speech of another the code functions of our own idiolect, his speech is intelligible to us. If the denotations of his words are altered so as to have little correspondence with the denotations of the phonologically like words in our own idiolect, or if the phonological shapes of his words with the same denotations are altered be-

---

[13]Two languages do, indeed, tend to become codes for the same concepts when they are both regularly spoken by largely the same people, as with a local vernacular and a national or regional standard language or, again, as with the kind of situation in the Northwest Amazon we have considered above. The convergence of two languages (Kannada and Marathi) toward common phonological and grammatical patterns and common denotations, together with retention of distinctive lexical forms, is reported for a largely bilingual village in India by Gumperz (1969). See also Gumperz and Wilson (1971).

yond our ability to recognize them, in either case mutual intelligibility is lost. Considerable variance is possible within these limits without such loss. Two people speak the "same" language, then, if the variance between their idiolects does not exceed these limits.

But this is not the end of the matter. The problem of definition is actually more complicated. When space technicians start talking about space technology or linguists start talking about technical matters pertaining to language, a layman finds himself unable to understand what is being said. Does this mean that the layman and space technician speak different languages? In one sense it does. The layman recognizes that he has to learn the "language" of space technology, the special vocabulary and the concepts that comprise its denotations. But in another sense, the layman and the specialist both speak English (or whatever), for they communicate readily about nontechnical matters; and even when he talks about his specialty, the space technician uses ordinary English words according to English grammar intermixed with a specialized vocabulary. There is obviously a difference between the situation where two people both have knowledge of similar subjects but cannot communicate with each other about them and the situation where they can communicate about subjects of which they both have knowledge but not about other subjects. In the former case, the two speak different languages; in the latter case they speak the "same" language, but with varying degrees of competence in the several subject matters for which it serves as a code.

LANGUAGE AND SOCIETY

The analogy between language and species as typological concepts is not the only one to be drawn between behavioral and biological phenomena. Biologists distinguish sharply between the genetic inheritance of an individual organism and the actual traits that it exhibits when it has reached maturity. The genetic inheritance consists of the chemical structure of the molecules in the chromosomes of the original cell (fertilized egg) from which the individual organism grew. The particular structures represented in the chromosomes make up the individual's genotype, and the physical characteristics of the mature organism make up its phenotype. The genotype is a plan or blueprint of what the individual will be; the phenotype is the material manifestation of that plan as influenced by the conditions in which the plan was realized.

Actually, each individual carries not one but two overall plans, because he inherits not one but two sets of chromosomes, one from each parent. Each chromosome contains molecules of DNA (deoxyribonucleic acid), each DNA molecule consisting of a chain of amino acids. Particular positions on this chain control particular aspects of heredity; each such position is called a **gene**. Variant characteristics possible for a given gene are called **alleles** of the gene. Corresponding genes on the corresponding chromosomes in the two sets may have identical alleles or different ones. Insofar as the alleles are identical, the two inherited plans are the same; but insofar as the alleles are different, the plans differ. The phenotype represents a resolution of the different potentialities of these two overall plans. The components of the two plans, however, remain distinct at the genetic level (in the individual's reproductive cells). Depending on which one of each pair of chromosomes is passed on by an individual to one of his offspring, the offspring will acquire one or the other set of plan components (alleles) carried by that pair of chromosomes. This set is then added to a corresponding but not identical set from the offspring's other parent to make up the offspring's genotype.

What interests us here is that in a given inbreeding population there is a range of alleles for each gene. No individual can carry more than two of them, but there can be many more than two carried within the population as a whole, the different alleles being brought together in a variety of combinations in the course of time. The total number of alleles for all genes in an inbreeding population constitutes what is called the **gene pool** of that population.

The gene pools of distinct populations differ both in the nature of the alleles represented and in the relative frequency of their occurrence. Thus the relative frequency of the alleles for the blood antigens O, A, and B differs from gene pool to gene pool, and some gene pools do not have the B allele represented in them at all. The relative frequency in the gene pool determines, according to the laws of probability, the relative frequency of the occurrence of the genotypes OO, OA, OB, AA, AB, and BB in the population at any given time, and these in turn determine the relative frequency of the actual blood types or phenotypes O (OO), A (OA, AA), B (OB, BB), and AB (AB) in the population.

Coming back to language, we must draw a parallel distinction between the plan or model, the set of principles for speaking, carried by a speaker and the utterances he actually makes. The latter are the concrete acoustical manifestations of that plan as influenced by the actual conditions in which the plan is realized, such as the inebriation of the speaker, his state of fatigue, etc.

It is tempting to equate this distinction between language as a plan and actual speech utterances with the distinction drawn by the French linguist de Saussure between what he called *langue* and *parole*. For him, however, *langue* was the ideal plan carried by a population as a collectivity, whereas *parole* was its imperfect manifestation both in actual speech and in the version of the plan carried by any one individual. Idiolects belonged to the domain of *parole*. Here, by contrast, we see each idiolect as a plan distinct from the utterances the individual makes. To be sure, each individual has a conception of an ideal plan that he projects on the collectivity. Moreover, there may be a version of an ideal plan on which certain recognized authorities in a society agree, and this may be what everyone else says is the ideal plan for the collectivity, the plan on which everyone ought to seek to pattern his idiolect. Some countries, including France, have a national academy one of whose tasks is to decide on the ideal plan, the particular set of standards that constitutes the standard national language. But even where such standardizing agencies exist, no two people can be completely of one mind regarding the plan. Even the recognized authorities debate with one another about it.

An individual, of course, can carry only two overall genetic plans in his genotype, whereas he can carry many different plans for speaking. Moreover, his phenotype represents a syncretistic resolution of the two plans of his genotype, whereas his speech may reflect a choice of one or another plan, segregated in his mind and in his habit structure as entirely distinct; or it may reflect some degree of syncretism among the several plans in his repertory, as when he starts a sentence in English and then injects French vocabulary into it. Because language is acquired by learning rather than by biological inheritance, there is no fixed number of discrete plans for speaking that a person may carry (or distinct languages he may know). Neither is there a fixed number of alternative subplans (styles of speaking) for some part of an overall plan that he may carry. For example, he may have alternative patterns of pronunciation of the same words, as with the vowel of the English words *fog, hog, log,* etc., pronounced either as in *mop* or as in *dog.* A speaker may switch from speaking according to the standards of one subplan to speaking according to the standards of another, depending on the company he is keeping and the impression he wishes to make, as when he shifts from saying *running, speaking, hearing* to saying *runnin', speakin', hearin'.* He may carry alternative words in his vocabulary for saying the same thing, using one or another depending on whether he is in mixed company or not.

As these examples suggest, a person may have a plan for shifting from using one set of words to using another set and for shifting from one phonological pattern to another. His selection of one subplan or another is governed by standards and can be said to have a "grammar" in that it is in accord with a master plan.[14] Similarly, one's selection of English, French, or Trukese—assuming one knows them all—may also be governed by a master plan. When a Frenchman who speaks English well gets up at a banquet in his honor in the United States and makes his after-dinner speech to his English-speaking audience in French rather than in English, he is communicating something by that selection. What he communicates depends on his and his hearers' standards governing the selection among languages in one's repertory in different social situations.

For any population, then, there is not only a pool of idiolects or individual versions of a language, there is also a pool of recognized variants or dialects and even a pool of distinct languages. Knowledge

---

[14]That there are standards governing the use of different styles of speaking, the use of different dialects, and even the use of different languages, as in the Northwest Amazon region, reminds us that it is often difficult to decide where language leaves off and the rest of culture begins. The study of standards governing styles of speaking and similar matters relating to the use of language has been aptly called "the ethnography of speaking" by Hymes (1962). For an introduction to the study of how different styles of speaking and different dialects are associated with particular social situations or social groups—a subject known as sociolinguistics—see Trudgill (1974). See also Burling (1970), Labov (1972), Rubin (1973), and Hymes (1974).

of these languages and dialects varies from individual to individual. Some individuals are monodialectal, and others are bi- or multidialectal; some are monolingual, and others are bi- or multilingual. Just as the number of alleles for different genes and their relative frequency in a population characterizes that population's genetic makeup, so the number of dialects and languages known by persons in a given population together with the relative frequency of persons who know them and the extent of their knowledge of them characterizes a population's linguistic makeup.

We cannot say what is *the* genotype or phenotype for any in-mating population, no matter how much certain phenotypic characteristics may be idealized in public by members of that population. But we can properly say what is its genetic and phenotypic makeup. In some populations the makeup may be monotypic for some genes, as where only the blood type O (genotype OO) is represented, but this is not the ordinary situation. Similarly, we can describe the linguistic makeup of a population, but we cannot always say that it is characterized by a single language or dialect, however much a particular dialect may be idealized in public by members of that population or even claimed by them as their dialect. Such claims are important, as we shall see, but they do not reflect the actual linguistic repertory of a population. Indeed, we cannot even say in many cases that a population has a particular language or dialect as the language or dialect "of the home." Having a particular language as the language of the home can serve as the basis for defining a population to begin with, just as having brown eyes can be used to define a population. If, however, we define a population by political, geographical, or social criteria instead of linguistic ones, then the best we can do is to characterize its linguistic makeup. Its makeup may be monolingual or monodialectal, but it probably will not be (Gumperz, 1962).

Any major city will illustrate the point. But so may a small village, as does any one of the longhouse villages of the Northwest Amazon, described earlier. On the other side of the world, the village of Galilo on the north coast of New Britain Island off New Guinea provides another example. In 1954 it had 248 locally resident inhabitants. All adult men of the village were at least bilingual in West Nakanai and Melanesian Pidgin English. Most of them also knew some Tolai, a language spoken around the city of Rabaul at the northeastern end of the island over 100 miles away. Tolai was taught in the local, mission-run school and was used in Protestant church services. A few men knew yet other languages. Fewer adult women were competent in Pidgin English, but many knew some Tolai, and all were fluent in West Nakanai. For all Galilo's inhabitants, West Nakanai had been the language of the home and hence the first language learned. They thought of West Nakanai as the "local language" or "our language." But there is more than one dialect of West Nakanai, as Galilo's residents were well aware. Many of them had spent various amounts of time living in villages where other dialects were prevalent; some had spent much of their childhood there. A few individuals regularly patterned at least some of their speech after usages associated with a dialect prevalent in another area. Even in its use of West Nakanai, Galilo was far from linguistically homogeneous.

Complicated as the linguistic makeup of a community may be, the different dialects and languages represented there are certain to play different roles and to be valued in different ways (Ferguson, 1959; Rubin, 1962). The nature of these roles varies from place to place, and generalizations about them are difficult to make. Already mentioned are the dialects and languages of the home, the first to which a child is exposed. The members of a community may all use the same language or dialect of the home, or they may not. Indeed, more than one dialect or language may even be spoken regularly in the same home.

There is almost certainly a language or dialect that is identified with the community or locality. It is the one cultivated by those who identify themselves with the locality. When more than one language is represented in a community—as is so often the case—the language identified with the locality is the one people are expected to use, if they can, when they engage in day-to-day, interfamilial transactions. It is the language in which everyone is expected to be competent.

In large political units, of course, there may be several local or regional languages. There is then almost certain to be a language of public administration. Where people from different localities with different local languages regularly trade with one another or have any other kind of regular social dealings, there will be a language of commerce of some kind. Any language whose role invites widespread competence in it across regional linguistic boundaries is likely to become established as a *lingua franca*, as has happened with Swahili in East Africa and with Pidgin English in New Guinea.

Although populations, we have seen, commonly have more than one language represented within them, it is also common everywhere to identify populations as such with particular languages, as far as possible. In practice, when we identify a population with a language, we select as *its* language the one with which the population identifies itself and that serves as its local interfamilial language. It may also be the official language of a state, or it may not be. It may be the local language of only one village or serve as the local language of many villages and towns in a wide region. We must hasten to add that some individuals may personally identify themselves with some other language in preference to what functions as the local language of their community, as when an immigrant continues to identify himself personally with the local language of the community from which he came, although he identifies another language with the community in which he now lives but in which he sees himself as a resident alien. When we speak of a person's native language, we usually also have in mind a local language, the one identified with the community where he first learned to speak. But we become unsure of just what to say if this was not also the private language of his home.[15]

The social organization of complex communities may work to segregate their populations into several distinct isolates. Within each of these isolates communication occurs in a wide variety of contexts, but between them it is confined to very few contexts. In a plantation community, for example, the owners and managers may deal with one another in many activities and interact frequently, and the workers may do likewise among themselves. But dealings between the managers and the workers may occur only in very few contexts, having to do with the conduct of work and the maintenance of order. Under such circum-

---

[15]We still lack a developed technical terminology for the major functional roles of languages. Widely used are expressions such as "vernacular," "standard language," "national language"; "language of the home," "trade language," "official language," "ritual language"; "high language" and "low language." Some of these terms are used in partly overlapping senses.

stances, the managerial and working communities are likely to exhibit dialect differences. In the aftermath of military conquest they may even be identified with different languages. Competence in different languages and dialects is closely associated with caste and class divisions in complex communities (see Burling, 1970, Chapter 8). In such a community, it may be difficult to say what is its local language.

Human societies, then, differ from one another in their linguistic makeup—in the languages and dialects in which their members have some competence and in the extent to which each of these languages and dialects is competently represented. The several languages and dialects in a society's language pool play different roles and are differently valued. According to the roles they play, there are different incentives and opportunities for the society's members to learn them. The extent of competence in any one language or dialect is a reflection of these incentives and opportunities. When masters and servants come from different segments of the larger society, for example, each with their own language, and the children of the masters grow and are educated apart from the children of the servants, then we can expect the servants to have greater competence in the language of their masters than the masters in the language of their servants. But if the children of the masters grow up in the care of the servants and play regularly with the servant's children, we can expect them as adult masters to be more competent in the language of the servants than the servants are in the language of their masters. Everyone has a very strong incentive to be competent in whatever language is the one in which day-to-day affairs between families are conducted in the local community. Hence it is the natural candidate as the language with which to identify the community.

But what can serve as the local language can change. If for some reason the people of Galilo village in New Britain, referred to above, should find reason to use Pidgin English increasingly in local day-to-day affairs at the expense of West Nakanai, Pidgin English would then replace West Nakanai as the local language. Competence in Pidgin English is widespread enough to make such a change a real possibility for Galilo. So far, the many interests of Galilo's residents have led them to continue to use West Nakanai as their local language. Galilo's linguistic evolution as a community depends on how circumstances will serve in the future to affect what Galilo's residents perceive as their interests. Their changing interests will affect the way they choose to use the several languages available to them in their language pool. Just this kind of change to Pidgin English took place in the Admiralty Islands, when Manus-speaking and Usiai-speaking people joined to form a new community (Schwartz, 1962). They formally decided that Pidgin English would thereafter be the language of public use, although Manus and Usiai might continue to be spoken in the privacy of the home.

Changes of this kind reveal that there is a selective process at work here, one that is not unlike natural selection in biological evolution, as Hymes (1961) has observed. In natural selection, a particular set of environmental circumstances differentially affects the survival and hence the reproductive possibilities of the various phenotypes and their associated genotypes in a population. Stability and change in these circumstances work, therefore, to maintain or alter the relative frequency of the several alleles of a gene in the population, according to their effect on the role each allele can play in an organism's functioning. Similarly, stability or change in the social environment of a community's members serves to maintain or alter the choices they make among the linguistic alternatives available to them for communication. Thus psychological selection, expressed in human choice of ends and of means to ends, serves to guide the course of a society's linguistic evolution.

We have been talking here of the linguistic evolution of a society or population isolate, something that must not be confused with the evolution of a language as a system of standards. Consideration of the latter must wait until we have examined language in relation to the individual speaker.

LANGUAGE AND THE INDIVIDUAL

Each individual, we have said, has his own idiolect—his own version of whatever language he speaks. It is not an exact replica of the idiolects of his fellows, but close enough to them so that he can talk effectively with them and they with him. A language is not something that people who speak it "perfectly" all perfectly share. There are as many versions of a language as there are speakers of it, as we discover when we begin to observe speech closely and record the many small differences we ordinarily ignore. The variance among these versions is quite small among adults for whom it is a first language; the variance is greater among children and among people for whom it is other than a first language. When a person can bring his version within the range of variance of adults for whom it is a first language, these adults are then likely to say that he speaks it "perfectly," by which they mean that they cannot distinguish him from themselves collectively (although they might well be able to distinguish him from any one of them individually).

From the point of view of an individual learning a language, the situation has a different look. There is a set of others who talk meaningfully to one another and who thus seem to "share" a language. There is something to be learned, a set of standards for speaking, and it is something the others already know. By using these others as his guide, the individual learner may some day manage to discover what those standards are and with practice be able to speak the way the others do.

The actual process of language learning is a complicated one that is still imperfectly understood. But we know that the individual learner plays an active role, the standards he arrives at for speaking and interpreting the speech of others being his own creation. Other people, of course, have their standards for him and correct him when he fails to meet them. But they do not recite to him the principles to which their own speech conforms. These principles are something they know only subjectively in that they have a feel for them. Unless they are grammarians, they have not objectified these principles to themselves. They know when someone's speech sounds queer or wrong, and they can tell him how they think he should have said it, but they can rarely tell him why, at least not accurately. People often have rules of thumb regarding their language, as well as regarding other aspects of their culture, but such rules seldom coincide with the principles to be inferred from an analysis of the patterns manifested in their behavior. That their language has a systematic structure that can be expressed as grammatical rules often comes as a startling revelation to people who serve as informants in linguistic research. For this reason, Edward Sapir (1927) used the expression "unconscious patterning" in reference to standards of speech behavior. For the individual learner, then, the task is not only to remember the specific corrections of his mistakes, but to generalize from them. The trick is to infer the patterns that others can illustrate but have difficulty describing. That children subjectively infer patterns for themselves in the course of language learning is clear from the kinds of mistakes they make, as when they overgeneralize or make wrong analogies (Brown and Bellugi, 1964; Ervin, 1964). A common mistake in English, for example, is the use of *brang* and *brung* for *brought* on the assumption that *bring* follows the pattern of *ring* and *sing*.

What the learner comes up with in the end is a feel for a set of patterns and, at the same time, a feel for principles by which to select among the patterns to construct actual utterances. He has developed these principles out of his experience of the behavior of others. He assumes that they all collectively know essentially the same thing and that what he knows is the same as what they know. For him the group has a language; and it is what he understands it to be, as long as the behavior of members of the group falls within the range of expectations provided by his standards for them. When he encounters behavior that does not meet his expectations, he concludes that he is dealing with a different dialect or language, something new to be learned.

More than one set of standards, however, can produce what appears to be the same kind of behavior. A pattern can be adequately conceptualized in more than one way. The subjective feel of two individuals for the same patterns can involve different criteria and principles, just as a color-blind person can learn to discriminate traffic signals by responding to contrasting features of the overall pattern that are not the ones used by people with normal vision. (For an example in phonology, see Sherzer, 1970.) However, so long as their different criteria and principles for speaking lead two persons to talk in ways that meet the expectations each has for the other, they have the sense that they share the same standards, that they speak the same language.

Just as the individual learner develops subjective and subconscious standards that he projects on his fellows, a linguist, who is himself just another individual learner, inevitably does the same thing. But he does it self-consciously and with the intention of objectifying to himself and to others—of formulating in words—the criteria and principles by which he discerns the patterns in the speech of those he studies. What results is a codification of the patterns he has discerned. For him and for those who accept his work, the standards he thus develops for others are a true representation of "their language." Their acceptance of his speech as like their own is the only test of the validity of his formulation. What he describes—the only thing he can describe—is his own formulation out of his own experience. It is not really their language, but a representation of the language he has created for them. Nevertheless, if it meets the criterion of acceptability when used as a guide to their speech behavior, we cannot say that it is wrong.

But the facts of a language—the points of contrast insisted on by its speakers and the ways these points of contrast are distributed with respect to one another—can be seen in terms of more than one pattern, as we have already indicated. Two linguists can produce different codifications, different statements of standards, for the speech of the same people. These two codifications can equally account for their speech behavior and, used as a guide, lead to nearly identical behavior. To ask which of these codifications is the "true" representation of the language is to assume the existence of a set of principles that is perfectly shared by others, an assumption that we cannot make, even though the perspective from which we are used to looking at language inclines us naturally to make it. We must accept that more than one valid representation of a language is possible. One representation may be more useful for some purposes and another more useful for others. Our choice among competing but valid representations will be governed by how well it serves our particular purposes. Each may give useful insights into different things.

The proposition that there can be in reality no one true formulation of the standards comprising a particular language has important implications for theory. It implies that the patterns of usage exhibited by speakers must involve a high degree of redundancy. The discriminations and linkages they require must be capable of being made in more than one way, using more than one particular set of criteria and, presumably, more than one particular combination of psychological aptitudes. Only thus, it seems, is it possible for humans to "share" a language at all. Cognitive sharing involves pragmatically productive approximations of understanding, not one-to-one correspondences of psychic organization. The characteristics of systems that are thus shared are constrained accordingly.

EVOLUTION OF LANGUAGES

A society's linguistic evolution, we observed, is to be sharply distinguished from the evolution of a particular language.[16] For the latter there are two considerations of primary importance. One is the matter we have just mentioned, namely that every individual creates his own version of a language in the course of learning it. The other is the different character and partial autonomy of the several major subsystems within a language.

Because each individual creates his own version of what he understands the language of his fellows to be, the degree to which his version approximates their individual versions must depend, aside from his own aptitude for learning, on the opportunities he has for discovering significant differences in his and his fellows' speech. The more he and they talk together and the wider the range of situations and of subject matters covered, the greater the opportunities to discover these differences and to adjust speech to reduce the variance.

Phonology, morphology, and syntax enter into all communications, regardless of subject matter, and are therefore likely to show less variance than will occur in the semantic and symbolic systems. The semantic system will show greater variance in the meanings of words that are little used and less variance in those that are commonly used. The symbolic system, similarly, will show greater variance in connection with words denoting things that people experience under widely differing circumstances, and it will tend to show less variance with

---

[16]Our concern here is not with the evolution of language in general from some earlier and less complicated animal signaling system—with the evolution, that is, of human communication (Greenberg, 1957, p. 65). Rather, it is with how the contents of particular languages evolve or change and how families of related languages come into being. Our concern, thus, is with micro- rather than macro-evolution—with the systematic aspect of change rather than with developmental stages.

words that denote things of which people have much common experience.

Whether the overall range of variance is great or small, its content is likely to shift in time, if for no other reason than the addition of new speakers and the loss of old ones. Some of these shifts may be random, but others may show certain tendencies that give direction to the course of change.

One observed tendency has to do with so-called irregularities and unusual constructions. If these irregularities occur in words and expressions that are frequently used, they persist in the language much longer than if they occur in words that are uncommon (Hockett, 1958, pp. 396-397). In Old English, for example, there was a class of nouns that underwent internal vowel modification in the plural form. Another class of nouns formed the plural by suffixing *-n* or *-en*. One by one, the nouns in these classes came to form their plural with the suffix *-s* (or *-es*) in accordance with one of the several patterns of plural formation that had become more common in Middle English. Now all that remains of these classes is to be found in very commonly used words or in words that were very commonly used until the industrial revolution. The plurals *men, women, teeth, feet, lice, mice,* and *oxen* are obvious examples. Such older forms as *kye, een,* and *shoon* have been replaced, however, by *cows, eyes,* and *shoes.*

The course of replacement in the latter instances was gradual among English speakers. By misplaced analogy with other forms, there was a tendency for new speakers of the language to say *shoes* instead of *shoon.* Some retained it uncorrected, and after a while there were two competing forms, just as today *dived* competes with *dove* as the past tense of *dive.* At some point one of the competing forms came to be seen as more refined, sophisticated, or modern and the other as quaint, rustic, low class, or old-fashioned.

Imperfect learning and misplaced analogy are not the only sources of competing forms. People often play with their language, introducing abbreviations and distortions deliberately. Metaphorical usage produces competing forms, for example, *kid* as a competing form for *child* in English. Word taboos also promote the coinage or borrowing of alternative forms, which may eventually replace older forms in ordinary usage, as in English *pee* was formed from the first letter of *piss,* which it replaced in many social contexts. And population movement, bringing together in the same community speakers of somewhat different dialects, gives rise to competing forms on a large scale.

Because his fellows do not all speak alike, the learner must choose, from among the competing forms and styles of speaking they present to him, the one after which he will model his own speech. To reduce the variance between his speech and that of some of his fellows, he must increase the variance between it and the speech of others. He must select from among his fellows those with whom he wishes to identify himself and with whom he wishes others to identify him. Those he chooses as his models or reference figures[17] may be his parents, a dominant member of his childhood playgroup, a charismatic leader in his community, or persons he considers high class.

Louis Giddings used to tell of a small Alaskan Eskimo community into which a family had moved from over the mountains where a different dialect of Eskimo was spoken. A son in this family became the leader of the children's playgroup in the community. Soon all the children were imitating this boy's dialect rather than that of their parents and there had developed a dialect cleavage in the community along generation lines. If the younger generation persisted in this choice, the community would in a generation's time end up with a different dialect as its local language.

This example illustrates how the selection of models for the self can produce a change of the sort we discussed in connection with the linguistic evolution of a community: a change as to which of two dialects represented in a community's language pool will come to function as its local language in everyday, interfamilial relations. Here the choice was between distinct competing traditions. But evolutionary change within a single tradition—within what we perceive as the same ongoing local language—involves the same process of choosing among competing forms (Hoenigswald, 1960). Here, however, the competing

---

[17]The term "reference group" is commonly used in sociological literature to indicate the group, class, or segment of society with which a person wishes to be identified and that he takes as his model for himself, or whose approval or acceptance he seeks for himself. Individuals can be just as important as groups in this regard. (See Hyman, 1968.)

forms are styles of pronouncing a particular phoneme (rather than two whole phonological systems), or they involve such things as pronouncing or dropping the final vowels of words, regularly putting an adjective before or after the noun it modifies, or consistently using a particular word in one or another competing sense (for example, the English verb *realize* in the sense of "understand" or in the sense of "make real").

Because language learning is a process of imperfectly approximating rather than perfectly duplicating the speech of others, there are bound to be competing forms, competing styles of pronunciation, and competing patterns of semantic and symbolic usage within what is perceived as a single, continuing, local language tradition. As each generation develops new reference figures, the central tendency within the range of idiolect variance will shift accordingly.

Characteristic of language change is a strong tendency for change to be consistent. In the language of the Gilbert Islands in the Pacific, for example, the phoneme /t/ was once pronounced much like English *t*, but without aspiration. Before the high front vowel /i/ it has come to be pronounced like English *s* in some dialects and like English *j* in others. The point is that this shift in pronunciation has not occurred only in some words where /t/ was followed by /i/; it has occurred in all of them. The change was carried all the way through. The change itself had a pattern. Such consistency characterizes phonological change in all languages, and it presumably characterizes change in other aspects of language as well. Language being itself a pattern of behavior, change in language is a change in pattern and is itself patterned.

Patterns, however, cross-cut one another. A consistent change in one pattern may have the effect of disrupting another one, fragmenting it into several distinct patterns or creating complexities and irregularities where there had been none before. These complexities and irregularities then become prime targets for the development of competing forms by analogy with patterns elsewhere in the language along the lines already discussed. The language of Truk will illustrate.

At one time, judging from related languages, all Trukese words ended in a vowel. There were, moreover, five vowel phonemes: /i/, /e/, /a/, /o/, /u/. How these vowels were pronounced varied predictably according to what other vowels immediately followed them: /a/ followed by /e/ in the next syllable was pronounced like the *a* of English *hat*; followed by /o/ in the next syllable it was pronounced something like the *aw* of English *law*; and followed by /a/ it was pronounced like the *a* of English *father*. A similar pattern still obtains in the related language of the Gilbert Islands. In time vowels at the end of words became shortened to a whisper and then were dropped entirely, being retained only in compounds, within words. What had originally been phonemically /faane/ ("building") and /faana/ ("under him") continued to preserve the distinctive pronunciation of the first vowels, although the subsequent vowels that accounted for that pronunciation were lost. These pronunciations, rather than the final vowels, were what now distinguished between the two words. They now marked significant points of contrast and functioned as distinct phonemes, /á/ in /fáán/ ("building") and /a/ in /faan/ ("under him"). Similarly what was /saapwo/ ("district") became phonemically /sóópw/. In this way the original five vowel phonemes in the ancestral language have become the nine vowel phonemes described above (footnote 6) of modern Trukese (Dyen, 1949). A systematic change in the handling of final vowels led to a complication in the number of significant points of contrast and to an increase in the number of vowel phonemes. But in all of this, consistency was maintained. The effect of a following /e/ or /o/ on a preceding /a/ was consistent phonetically before the loss of final vowels and was consistent phonemically after the loss of final vowels.

Consistency in change has a most important consequence. It produces regular patterns of correspondence between related languages. If every instance of an old phoneme /a/ has become /á/ in Trukese where it was once followed by an old /e/ but has remained /a/ in Trukese where it was once followed by an old /a/, we would expect instances of /aCe/ (C here representing any consonant) in a related language (where final vowels were not lost) to correspond consistently to instances of Trukese /á/, and instances of /aCa/ to correspond to instances of Trukese /a/. This is just what we find when we compare Gilbertese and other Pacific languages with Trukese. Such systematic correspondence of the phonemes of words of similar meaning in different languages is the most important single piece of evidence that the languages represent traditions stemming from a once common ancestral language. They have changed in the course of time, each one in its own way, but the retention of pattern, which gives consistency even to change, is reflected in the regular correspondences. Just such correspondences provided the basis for the historically famous Grimm's Law, which stated systematically the correspondence of consonants between Low and High German and the older Indo-European languages, such as Sanskrit and Ancient Greek.[18] As related languages continue to change in the course of time, the patterns of correspondence become increasingly less obvious and require more careful examination to uncover, but they continue to be there. Thus it has been possible to discover what languages go together in language families or stocks, a discovery that has laid the foundations for much of our understanding of the nature of language in general and of the ways in which languages change. (For processes of change in language, see Sapir, 1921; Hockett, 1958; Hoenigswald, 1960; Weinreich, Labov, and Herzog, 1968; Lehman, 1973; and Bynon, 1977.)

PIDGIN AND CREOLE LANGUAGES

Languages evolve and give rise to language families in the ways outlined earlier in this chapter when there is un unbroken chain of successive generations of speakers for whom these were the first languages learned and the languages in which they first gained the fluency expected of all native-born adult speakers. A language may also have continuity as a tradition when it is a second language for significant numbers of speakers whose opportunity for developing fluency equivalent to that of native speakers is severely limited. Under such conditions, a distinctive form of the language emerges. How much it differs from the parent language as spoken by native speakers depends on the nature and extent

---

[18] For example, the initial consonants of Ancient Greek and English correspond in the following manner:

English			Greek		
p	t	k	b	d	g
b	d	g	ph	th	kh
f	th	h	p	t	k

Compare, for example: English *tame, tree, two* and Greek *damazō, doru, duo;* English *daughter, deer, door* and Greek *thugatēr, thēr* (wild animal), *thura;* English *thatch, thy, three* and Greek *tegos, teos, treis.*

of the constraints on learning. When the differences are marked, we speak of the emergent language (or dialect) as a pidgin or creole. If it remains a second language for all of its speakers (including native speakers of the parent language) and is used in limited contexts, it is technically a **pidgin**. If it becomes the first language of a group of people who pass it on to their children as such, with elaboration suitable to the needs of the many contexts of community life, it is technically a **creole**.

What gives rise to pidgins is the situation in which people who speak mutually unintelligible languages begin to have frequently recurring dealings with one another. If only two languages are involved, the native speakers of each may seriously try to learn the other. Usually, however, even with only two languages, the burden of learning falls less heavily on the speakers of one language and more heavily on speakers of the other (or others). The language of the people who are under less pressure to learn becomes, then, the target language that the others must learn.

If the social contexts for which a *lingua franca* is needed are limited—to markets or to plantation work, for example—and if the motivation and opportunity for learning does not exceed the practical requirements of these contexts, what emerges is a stripped-down version of the language being learned. Its vocabulary will be drawn very largely from that of the target language, but its phonology is likely to reflect the prior speech habits of its new learners, who speak it with a "thick accent." Native speakers of the target language, moreover, already have established habits for simplifying their language for foreigners, modeled on the two- and three-word sentences of their own small children (Slobin, 1977). Accordingly, they present their language to the new learners in a form that is greatly simplified grammatically. If the new learners are of diverse linguistic background, they will use the target language in the simplified form in which they are learning it as a *lingua franca* among themselves as well as to communicate with its native speakers. Thus a pidgin comes into being. It is a *lingua franca* that has no native speakers; that is, no speakers for whom it is a first language.

If the pidgin speakers live apart from their native communities (as a group of plantation workers, for example), and bear children who associate with native speakers of the target language and with one another in the plantation setting, what began as a pidgin will become elaborated as a creole. The direction of elaboration will depend on the extent to which the target language continues to be an important part of the linguistic environment. For example, English remained predominant in the English speaking parts of the Caribbean, where there is now almost a continuum from an extremely pidginized form of English at one end to something close to standard British English at the other end, with several gradations in between (Bickerton, 1975). Where the target language ceases to be an important part of the linguistic environment, the emerging creole will evolve like any other language, but without further influence from the original target language.

Pidgins are interesting because they show direct continuity of tradition from the target language, primarily in vocabulary or lexicon as a set of behavioral forms. Phonological change as a result of imperfect learning will tend to be systematic in the same way that such change is systematic under other conditions. The change will be greater within a shorter space of time, but continuity of formal lexical tradition will not be broken. The semantic tradition encoded by the lexical forms, however, may come largely from other sources. Thus, Melanesian Pidgin English as spoken in Papua New Guinea (now known as Neo-Melanesian) has a vocabulary that is derived almost entirely from English in its forms, but semantically the language is used in ways that correspond more closely to the semantic traditions of Malayo-Polynesian languages spoken in Papua New Guinea.[19]

Because the lexical tradition of Neo-Melanesian is formally English, the standard procedures by which languages are classified into linguistic families lead to the firm conclusion that Neo-Melanesian is a Germanic language within the Indo-European family and that its nearest linguistic relative is English. Because the continuity of tradition, however, was not as a first language but as a second language for a significant length of time, it has undergone a kind and degree of change that is different

---

[19] At least 85% of the entries in Murphy's (1954) dictionary are from English. Lincoln (1975) similarly finds that over 90% of the vocabulary of Bislama (Pidgin English as spoken in New Hebrides) is from English. He also finds that parallelisms in meaning and syntax are substantially greater between Bislama and Tangoan (a local Melanesian language) than between Bislama and English.

from that characterizing continuity of tradition without interruption as a first language. It may seem strange to classify Neo-Melanesian as a Germanic language, given our tendency to regard pidgins as not quite "proper" languages. Nevertheless, there are undoubtedly other languages that we accept as Indo-European without hesitation although they came into being in unrecorded history as a result of pidginization and subsequent creolization.

Among Malayo-Polynesian languages, also, those spoken in the Pacific Islands all share a large number of phonological and grammatical simplifications compared to related languages in Indonesia and the Philippines. These simplifications could have arisen among the ancestors of the Pacific Islanders for more than one reason; but their nature and extent is not incommensurate with what we find when we compare English creoles with more "standard" forms of English. It is quite possible that the ancestral language from which the many Malayo-Polynesian languages in the Pacific are descended was itself a pidginized form of an old Malayo-Polynesian that was widely used in trade in the eastern reaches of Indonesia and that became established as a creole among the seafaring traders whose activities led to the settlement of the Pacific. In any event, we must assume that the development of pidgins and creoles is not a new phenomenon but has been going on as a normal process in human history since the emergence of commerce and complex societies.

The process of pidginization requires us to recognize that the several systems of organization making up a language can have independent, or at least semi-independent continuities through time. The phonological, morphological and lexical, syntactic, and semantic systems are relatively autonomous traditions. They are all transmitted together when they are learned as a first language by so-called native speakers. But when second language learning occurs, the lexical system is the most readily learned as a set of behavioral forms, and it may have continuity as a tradition while being mapped largely onto the phonological, syntactic, and semantic traditions associated with the learners' first language. The resulting language belongs to the language family from which its lexical and morphological tradition comes, but we speak of it as having a substratum that reflects other antecedents. The substratum is evident mainly in phonology and syntax. As Neo-Melanesian demonstrates, moreover, the semantic system—the ideas that the language encodes—may have its continuity of tradition largely from the substratum language, as well. (For more on pidgins and creoles, see Burling, 1970 (pp. 169-188), and Trudgill, 1974 (pp. 166-174); and for fuller discussion, see Hall, 1965; Hymes, 1971; Mühlhäusler, 1974; and Valdman, 1977.)

Chapter 4

PROBLEMS IN THE CONCEPTION OF CULTURE

Our discussion of language has developed the point of view with which we shall now consider culture and its relation to the individual and to society. But before we apply this point of view to culture, we must observe that the term "culture" has acquired several different meanings in the last one hundred years. These several meanings reflect different assumptions about human evolution, different foci of interest (such as society, knowledge, and behavior), and different epistemological assumptions. (See the review by Kroeber and Kluckhohn, 1952.)

The term itself came into anthropological use from the German word *Kultur*. The better educated classes of Europe were presumed to be less ignorant than lowly peasants and country bumpkins and to have a greater understanding of the truth and a greater appreciation of the finer things of life. They were "more civilized." The degree to which people differed in their customs, beliefs, and arts from sophisticated Europeans was a measure of how ignorant and uncivilized they were. Human history was conceived as a steady rise from a state of primitive ignorance to one of progressively greater enlightenment as expressed in the increasingly complicated achievements of men in technology, material standard of living, medicine, political management, and the literary and other arts, and in an increasingly enlightened moral code. What made these achievements possible was greater knowledge of the "truth," both natural and moral. Knowledge of the truth was cumulative through time, steadily replacing superstition and ignorance. Its increase was the measure of human progress from savagery to civilization. The more of it a society possessed and manifested in its works, the more *Kultur* it had and the more civilized or cultured its members were—its elite members, at least. E. B. Tylor (1903, p. 1) was expressing very much this view in his much quoted definition of culture as "that complex whole which includes knowledge, belief, art, morals, law, custom, and any other capabilities and habits acquired by man as a member of society."

In this view, societies did not have discrete cultures but a greater or lesser share in the degree of general culture so far created and developed by mankind as a whole. The object of cultural anthropology was to try to reconstruct the steps or stages that had marked the growth of culture. Societies with the simplest technologies and the least elaborate political orders presumably represented the lowest stage of growth; others represented various intermediate stages; while western European societies, politically and militarily dominating the rest of the world in the nineteenth century, represented the most advanced stage.[20] In Tylor's words (1903, pp. 26-27), "By simply placing nations at one end of the social series and savage tribes at the other, arranging the rest of mankind between these limits . . . ethnographers are able to set up at least a rough scale of civilization—a transition from the savage state to our own."

At the end of the nineteenth century, Franz Boas began to use "culture" to refer to the distinctive body of customs, beliefs, and social institutions that seemed to characterize each separate society (Stocking, 1966). Instead of different societies having different degrees of culture or different stages of cultural development, each society had

---

[20] This view of human history was taken for granted by nineteenth-century intellectuals, including Karl Marx and his disciples. The latter incorporated into Communist dogma the major formulation of social evolutionary stages of the later nineteenth century, made by the great pioneering American anthropologist Lewis H. Morgan (1878). It is a paradox that modern Communism, which claims to champion the aspirations for social equality of the technically less industrialized nations, should still hold as dogma this arrogantly ethnocentric theory developed by the imperial elites of the nineteenth century.

a culture of its own. This usage became and continues to be the prevailing one in American anthropology, which has been strongly influenced in its development by Boas's students. Culture was still seen as composed of the things in Tylor's definition, but each society's particular practices, beliefs, and life style were to be examined as a unique entity that was unlike any other. New members of a community learned that community's culture from their fellows, just as they learned its language. Language and culture went together as a body of distinctive things about a community that were transmitted by learning and that gave to each community its own peculiar linguistic and cultural tradition.

Since each tradition was transmitted by learning, and since opportunities to learn depended on social contacts, the present content of any particular tradition (any particular society's culture) was to be explained in part, at least, by past exposures of the community to people carrying other traditions. These exposures provided opportunities for learning new things and incorporating them into the local tradition. Along with local environmental conditions, they were said to account for the unique combination of "traits" in each society's culture. Cultural differences were to be understood, therefore, as a result of the accidents of history and the limitations of environment rather than as a reflection of evolutionary stages and a presumed general law of evolutionary growth through which all societies were destined to pass (except as they were helped forward or "uplifted" by those that had already passed through ahead of them). (For an expression of this view, see Kroeber, 1948a.)

We shall not discuss here the relative merits of the so-called "evolutionary" and "historical" theories of cultural differences. (For extended reviews from different points of view, see Harris, 1968; Voget, 1975; and Honigmann, 1976.) Both theories agreed that culture, in either sense of the term, is learned and forms a body of tradition within any society. Their modern proponents agree, moreover, that all cultures are very complex, even among people whose technologies seem very simple by western industrial standards. This complexity, they also agree, follows directly from the tremendous potentiality that is provided by every known human language for objectifying and analyzing experience and for storing and retrieving information. Without language, the human ability to maintain and transmit a body of tradition would be minimal.[21] A number of ambiguities remain, however, as to just what we mean when we talk about a society's culture.

CULTURE VS. CULTURAL ARTIFACTS

A major difficulty has been failure to stick with the implications of the idea that culture is learned. Anthropologists have debated whether or not culture includes the things people make, such as their tools, bridges, roads, houses, and works of art, all the things to which they commonly refer as "material culture." But the material objects people create are not in and of themselves things they learn. Through their experience of the things their fellows have made, people form conceptions of them, learn how to use them, and discover how to make things like them. What they learn are the necessary percepts, concepts, recipes, and skills—the things they need to know in order to make things that will meet the standards of their fellows. The parallel with language is clear. Through their experience of other people's utterances, people learn a language; but the language is not the utterances. It is the percepts, concepts, recipes, and skills by which to make utterances that others will accept as meeting their standards. Such is what is learned; and what has been learned must be clearly distinguished from its material manifestations in manufactured products, overt behavior (including speech), and social events.

Here, then, we shall reserve the term **culture** for what is learned, for the things one needs to know in order to meet the standards of others. And we shall refer to the material manifestations of what is learned as **cultural artifacts**.

The importance of the distinction is readily apparent when we look at something like a West African mask or a Plains Indian medicine bundle in a museum. What we see and how we react to it is not what a

---

[21] Studies of monkeys and apes show that they are able to develop and transmit rudimentary customary behaviors, such as washing food before eating it and catching termites by poking straws into their holes and waiting for them to crawl up on the straws. But such is the extent of complexity of tradition among them.

West African or a Plains Indian sees or how he reacts to it. As material entities the mask and medicine bundle have not changed, but what they are in the eye of the beholder depends on the experience of the beholder—the things he has learned. Thus we see that the cultural differences among people are not simply in the things they behold but in the standards by which they behold them. Their different standards will lead them to create what are clearly differently formed things; but once created, these things—like mountains, lakes, and rivers—are features of the environment. How people respond to them and what they do with them indicates how they conceive of them, what they believe about them, how they value them, and what their principles are for using them.

Cultural artifacts are not limited to the material objects people produce. They may be social and ideological as well as material. Each new state of the United States is a human creation conforming to American cultural standards for state organization. Thus it manifests important features of American political culture. Once created, it becomes a feature of the environment to be dealt with as such, as every taxpayer knows. As this example suggests, the distinction between a culture and its artifacts can often be a tricky one to make. For instance, when we talk of a "way of life," at one moment we may be speaking of standards for doing things, and at the next moment we may be referring to the physical and social arrangements and to the organizations of activity that result when people apply these standards to implement their purposes. We must recognize that any cultural artifact, once created, may become a model for the creation of other artifacts, the idea of it being added to the body of standards in the culture. A striking utterance gives rise to a cliché of the language; the first sonnets become the prototype for a new literary form; and the teaching of a prophet is converted into an ethical standard. There is, thus, a feedback relationship between a culture and its artifacts that can easily confuse the necessary distinction between them.

THE "SHARED"-"LEARNED" DILEMMA

In the foregoing we have expressed a view that places culture in the minds and hearts of men. We cannot, of course, see into minds and hearts. But all of us attribute things to them in order to make behavior intelligible. There are some social and behavioral scientists, including some anthropologists, who choose not to recognize this, at least not for scientific purposes. One can sympathize with their reasons for doing so. For if culture is in the minds of men and if culture is also something shared by or common to the members of a society, then it becomes apparently necessary to postulate the existence of a collective mind and to see culture as consisting of what French sociologists have called "collective representations"; or we must apparently assume that others are capable of some kind of mystical mental communion in which we, as observers, are unable to participate. Certainly, it is unsound to attribute generally to others mental processes that individually none of us has been able to discover in himself.

One way out of the problem, that taken by cultural and behavioral materialists, is to disallow reference to minds in the definition and theory of language and culture. Culture is equated with behavior and not with the standards that govern behavior. It consists of the things we see people do and of the statistical patterning of events as we see them occur in a given community.[22] From this viewpoint, of course, communities of bees and ants may be said to have cultures, for there are discernible patterns of behavior that characterize events within them. Whatever is responsible for these patterns, however, seems to be transmitted largely through biological heredity rather than through learning. Therefore we do not recognize these patterns among bees and ants as cultural. But as soon as we include learning as essential to the definition of culture, we are confronted once again with mind—unless we confine our conception of learning to conditioned behavioral reflexes. For the products of learning include concepts, beliefs, preferences, principles, and standards, all things that we traditionally associate with mind. It may be tempting, therefore, to follow those anthropologists who say that the scientific study of culture, since it is concerned with the patterns characterizing groups, should confine itself to phenomena at the group level of abstraction. How individuals

---

[22] This view is elaborated by Marvin Harris (1964) and provides the basis for his extended commentary on anthropological theory (1968).

relate to these patterns and how the process of learning works is a problem for psychology and not for anthropology.

Those who take this position necessarily beg the question of how we as individual observers and describers of cultures learn how to distinguish the significant from the nonsignificant in the behavior we observe and how we come to understand the meaning of what we describe; for even the strictest behavioral materialist is selective about what he records and makes assumptions about the meanings of things in his descriptions of events. Problems of method in science, after all, have to do with how scientists relate to the subject matters they study. If culture is learned, the problem of method is the problem of how scientists learn cultures in order to be able to describe them. The relation of the individual to culture is, therefore, crucial to method and theory in cultural anthropology.

The problem has been highlighted by Geertz, who from quite another perspective has taken issue with the position that culture is located in human minds. To refute this idea he has taken the example of a Beethoven quartet as an item of Western culture, and asserts that "no one would, I think, identify it with its score, with the skills and knowledge needed to play it, with the understanding of it possessed by its performers or auditors, nor, to take care, *en passant*, of the reductionists and reifiers, with a particular performance of it or with some mysterious entity transcending material existence" (1973, p. 11). He states further that "a Beethoven quartet is a temporally developed tonal structure, a coherent sequence of modeled sound—in a word music—and not anybody's knowledge of or belief about anything, including how to play it" (1973, pp. 11-12).

Of course, it can be so viewed. Reflection reminds us, however, that as an item of culture a Beethoven quartet is an abstraction in the minds of each of us who has any familiarity with it. It was conceived as a tonal structure in the mind of Beethoven in accordance with the musical standards of his day (as he understood them) for creating such structures and with an interest in how those standards might be stretched or modified (especially in his late quartets). What he conceived he made available to others by writing a score. Musicians must each individually interpret that score in an effort to recreate what they think, or would like to think, Beethoven had in mind when he wrote it. No two performances are identical, nor is the same performance identical in what any two performers or listeners apprehend it to be. The quartet, as a structure, exists in each individual's comprehension of it. We share the quartet at a performance, or, if we have learned enough about music, through reading the score, but what we share is exposure to an artifact of Beethoven's conception. What that artifact is as music depends on what the knowledge and skill and sentiments of each of us tells us it is.

Geertz's example reveals how much we need to take a critical look at the traditional anthropological view that culture pertains to and characterizes a community or society as distinct from the individual (is something common to and shared by a society's members) and at the same time is something that is learned. On the face of it, these are mutually incompatible propositions.

People learn as individuals. Therefore, if culture is learned, its ultimate locus must be in individuals rather than in groups. If we accept this, then cultural theory must explain in what sense we can speak of culture as being shared or as the property of groups at all, and it must explain what the processes are by which such "sharing" arises. It is not enough to deal with the problem by simply asserting that "shared culture" is only an analytical construct, as some anthropologists have done. We must go on to try to explain how this analytically useful construct relates to human phenomena, including the social and psychological processes that characterize humans in groups. It was with this goal in mind that we discussed the relation of language to society and to the individual, for "shared language" is also an analytical construct. The point of view expressed in that discussion is one we shall continue to elaborate in relation to culture.

THE PROBLEM OF PREDICTION

Before we move on to consider the content of culture, we must clarify another matter about which there is frequent misunderstanding. It concerns the role of prediction in cultural and behavioral science and arises as a problem out of concern with behavior and events as distinct from the things people learn—as distinct, that is, from standards for behaving and for interpreting events. Because prediction plays a crucial role in verifying the adequacy of scientific formulations, if one takes the approach of the behavioral materialists that culture is to be equated with behavior, it follows that the validity of a cultural description depends on its ability to predict behavior, to predict what people will actually do in given circumstances. To the extent that it is possible, such prediction is, of course, a universal human concern. Everyone is engaged in the game of predicting what his fellows will do or not do. But people who operate with what appears to be the same culture and who know one another personally very well are still unable perfectly to predict one another's behavior. Culture provides a set of expectations regarding what kinds of behavior are suitable in given situations; but only in highly ritualized situations, where suitable options are minimal, is it possible to predict the precise behavior. Then, too, people willfully violate the expectations a culture provides. It seems evident, therefore, that culture is not an instrument for predicting behavior precisely at all, although as a set of standards for behavior, culture helps to make behavior much more predictable than it would otherwise be.

In this respect, the example of language is again pertinent. None of us would claim that a description of a language can be scientifically valid only if it accurately predicts what any speaker of that language will actually say, including his slips of the tongue, in response to any particular stimulus. As was evident in our discussion of language, there are other things to be predicted. A scientifically valid account of a language is one that enables us to predict whether or not any particular utterance will be accepted by the language's speakers as conforming to their standards for speaking.[23] We similarly take the position that a valid description of a culture as something learned is one that predicts whether or not any particular action will be accepted by those who know the culture as conforming to their standards of conduct. Such prediction is very different from predicting what specific behavior will in fact occur.

By way of example, think of the game of American football. Those actively engaged in a game wish to predict as precisely as possible just what their opponents will do on each play. The captain for the

---

[23]Particularly telling in rebuttal of the strict behaviorist position is Chomsky's review (1959).

defense assesses the probabilities as he understands them and calls a defensive maneuver accordingly. In spite of his expertise, his predictive success is far from perfect, even for the limited range of offensive possibilities available to the other team. Each side tries to give the impression to the other side that it regularly does certain kinds of things under certain conditions, and having gotten its opponents predicting accordingly, proceeds to fool them by doing something different. The statistically unusual but highly successful play is unexpected, but it does not therefore violate the players' standards for what constitutes proper football. In learning to play football, one has first to learn the rules of the game, which state the limits within which behavior is acceptable and beyond which it is not. One has also to develop certain physical skills in running, passing, catching, blocking, and tackling. Finally one has to learn offensive plays, which comprise a set of standard formulas or recipes for gaining ground toward a score, and one has to learn defensive plays for stopping them. Coaches can devise new formations and plays to their hearts' content as long as they keep within the rules of the game. A person who knows the rules can predict with great accuracy whether a particular play or action will be judged as violating them, but this knowledge will not enable him to predict what particular play will be used in a particular situation. A valid description of football is an account of what one needs to know to play it acceptably and to follow the game with understanding; it does not seek to predict how people will exercise their options within the rules in every conceivable situation. Coaches and quarterbacks, experts in the game, wish they could do this. They watch movies of their opponents in past games in order to discover the patterns of probabilities that characterize their styles of play within the rules. But someone exposed to the game of football for the first time is uninterested in such niceties. He wants to know what is necessary to follow the game with understanding.

There are, then, two orders of phenomena toward which prediction is directed in human behavior. One pertains to actual behavior and the other to standards for behavior. A system of standards for behavior—a culture—is an important aid in making predictions about actual behavior, but it is not of the same order as the behavior it helps predict. Culture allows people to predict that certain kinds of behavior and events are highly improbable, being in violation of standards; and it enables people to narrow the range of probabilities to a few alternatives. However, within the framework of expectations thus provided, the prediction of actual behavior and events is a statement of probabilities based on the percentages observed for a sample of past events regarding two kinds of things: what actually occurred and whether what occurred was in keeping with the standards or in violation of them. Some people cheat more often than others do, for example. For those who already know the standards, the rules of the game, this is the kind of prediction that is interesting.

The other order of phenomena to which prediction pertains has to do with what, among the things that might occur, will be acceptable according to people's standards for behaving. Here prediction is aimed not at what will happen but at what the standards are. It specifies what are the kinds of social, material, and behavioral units involved in events and what are the limitations on the ways in which they can be appropriately combined. In short, it is a statement of definitions and rules. To describe a language or a culture is to make a predictive statement of this latter kind. Both language and culture thus belong to the same order of phenomena, language being, of course, a part of culture, as Sapir (1929) has observed.[24]

CULTURE AND UNITS OF BEHAVIOR

In the sciences that do not deal with the behavior of living organisms, the observer makes as detailed a record as he can of what he thinks he sees. He abstracts patterns from a sample of such records, formulates hypotheses about the interrelations of different phenomena within these records, and makes predictions from the hypotheses as to what will happen under particular conditions. He waits for the conditions to occur or tries to create them artificially in the laboratory. If his predic-

---

[24] The inclusion of language within culture is not belied by the considerable autonomy languages display—at least in their phonological, morphological, and syntactic systems—from other parts of culture. Systems of etiquette, religious belief, technology, and family organization all display similar degrees of autonomy, to say nothing of games.

tions are met, he regards his constructions and hypotheses as verified. There are times when the appropriateness of the units of observation comes into question, as when they are not fine-grained enough. But in the behavioral sciences, especially in those dealing with human behavior, the appropriateness of units is a matter of crucial concern. Suppose you are the proverbial man from Mars making a study of American football. You watch several games and make a detailed record of everything you think you see happening. You analyze this record for all the statistical patterns you can find in it. But you never ask anyone to explain the game to you. You do not know what its object is, what the different team positions are or the constraints on what they can do, the system of downs, or any of the other rules of the game. You don't know what things in your record are relevant to the game and what things are irrelevant, such as a fist fight that develops between two players. You describe all kinds of activity but not the game of football.

The distinction we drew between emics and etics in connection with language is fully applicable here. Observation must be supplemented by some kind of helping response from those who already know the game (even if no more than approving and disapproving nods and shakes of the head) in order to sift the relevant from the irrelevant. Once we know what is relevant and what are the rules or standards governing it, then we know what are the units in terms of which to make statistical records of events. We can count first downs, off-side penalties, etc., but first we have to know what a first down or off-side penalty is. In the social sciences, we count all kinds of things like votes, sales, dollars, and occupations; but all of these things are significant units in a complicated game of living. We cannot count them if we cannot recognize them; and before we can recognize them, we have to know the standards and the rules of the game. To make predictive statements about actual behavior, we must first know the culture of which that behavior is an expression.

These considerations, taken with what was said about the shared-learned dilemma, can help to clarify the difference between our position about the nature of culture and that taken by Geertz (1973, pp. 10-13), a difference to which we have already called attention. Geertz stresses that human behavior must be viewed as "symbolic action," and culture is what it means. "Culture is public because meaning is," he says (1973, p. 12).

Knowing how to wink, Geertz asserts and we agree, is not the same as the physical act of winking. Not the same, either, is knowing how to interpret winks as symbolic acts. It is the existence of the knowledge of how to interpret them, on the other hand, that makes them symbolic acts. For Geertz, culture is both the acts as symbols and their meaning. He focuses on the artifacts—exposure to artifacts is what people share— and states that these artifacts as public symbols and the public meaning they have acquired in social exchanges constitute culture. We take the position that culture consists of the criteria people use to discern the artifacts as having distinctive forms and the criteria people use to attribute meaning to them. We address the problem of how these criteria, which are individually learned in social exchanges, can be said to be public at all, a problem Geertz does not address.

If we stop where Geertz does, we cannot readily account for the fact that people experience novel events and find them immediately mean- ingful, like a newly devised trick play in football or a newly created poem or musical composition. Our approach goes further and is con- cerned with the cognitive and emotional factors that make it possible for the novel to be meaningful. These factors, which form the ultimate locus of culture, help explain how culture as Geertz defines it can exist at all. Indeed, we are as concerned as he is with what is public; but we do not take it as given and simply to be described; we take it as a phenomenon to be explained.

Chapter 5

THE CONTENT OF CULTURE

We expect the content of culture to have clear parallels with the content of language, a language itself being a kind of cultural system. Students of language, we saw, have concentrated on speech forms (phonology and morphology) and on the principles of ordering them into intelligible utterances (syntax). They have paid much less attention to the content of semantic and symbolic systems. This concentration has resulted from taking behavior as the object of study. Such emphasis made it natural to focus on the morphology and syntax of speech behavior and not on the morphology and cognitive ordering of associated nonbehavioral phenomena. But in considering the content of culture we must take account of the entire range of phenomena—behavioral and nonbehavioral alike—that enter into human experience and that are the subject matter of learning. To be sure, other kinds of behavior than speech also have morphology, syntax, and meaning, as anthropologists are demonstrating,[25] but in the broader view we must now take, we shall find that culture contains other features in addition to the ones observed for language.

---

[25]For examples, see Birdwhistell (1953, 1970), W. Goodenough (1965), Hall (1959), Keesing (1970a), and Metzger and Williams (1963). See also Turner (1967, 1969).

Looking at culture as a product of human learning, I once summarized its content as follows:

1. The ways in which people have organized their experience of the real world so as to give it structure as a phenomenal world of forms, that is, their percepts and concepts.

2. The ways in which people have organized their experience of their phenomenal world so as to give it structure as a system of cause and effect relationships, that is, the propositions and beliefs by which they explain events and design tactics for accomplishing their purposes.

3. The ways in which people have organized their experience of their phenomenal world so as to structure its various arrangements in hierarchies of preferences, that is, their value or sentiment systems. These provide the principles for selecting and establishing purposes and for keeping oneself purposefully oriented in a changing phenomenal world.

4. The ways in which people have organized their experience of their past efforts to accomplish recurring purposes into operational procedures for accomplishing these purposes in the future, that is, a set of "grammatical" principles of action and a series of recipes for accomplishing particular ends. They include operational procedures for dealing with people as well as for dealing with material things.

   Culture, then, consists of standards for deciding what is, standards for deciding what can be, standards for deciding how one feels about it, standards for deciding what to do about it, and standards for deciding how to go about doing it. (W. Goodenough, 1963, pp. 258-259.)

The above summary serves as a point of departure only. It makes no mention of language or of rules and social obligations. It says nothing of customs and institutions. But its emphasis on standards points us in the direction we wish to go. We proceed, then, to consider these matters in greater detail under the following headings: forms, propositions, beliefs, values, rules and public values, recipes, routines and customs, systems of customs, and meaning and function.

FORMS

No one can treat every sensory experience from moment to moment as if it were unique, for then past experience would be of no help in dealing with the present. Of necessity people treat present experiences as like old ones, discriminating among them as they find such discrimination useful. The human approach to experience is categorical.

Fundamental to every individual's organization of experience, therefore, is a catalogue of forms or form categories that he has learned to discern directly with his senses. There are color categories, shape categories, taste categories, and so on. Combinations of these categories—this shape with that color, for example—define other categories in our catalogue of forms, such as oatmeal, ships, and roses. We also categorize the ways the things we discern appear to be mutually arranged and the ways they can become transformed as their mutual arrangements change.

Such discerned categories of phenomena and process are conceptual or ideal forms. They are defined as forms by whatever allows us to distinguish our experiences of them from one another, that is, by some set of distinctive features. We have already seen this in relation to language, whose distinctive features are the perceptual variables by which one linguistic form is distinguished as such from another. Examples for other aspects of culture are harder to find, because efforts to make emic descriptions of cultural forms are still largely exploratory.[26]

An important question concerns the extent to which the selection of distinctive features is governed by biologically built-in properties of our sensory equipment as against the extent to which selection is random.

---

[26]The term "ethnoscience" is frequently used in reference to this exploratory work. The interested reader should refer to Romney and D'Andrade (1964), Tyler (1969), Berlin and Kay (1969), Witherspoon (1971), Berlin, Breedlove, and Raven (1974), Hunn (1977), and Meigs (1977).

The real world seems to be full of all kinds of discontinuities quite apart from our sensory relationship to them. Our sensory equipment also has discontinuities, so that it can only serve as a filter, at best. We must assume, therefore, that there are some kinds of discriminations that people almost inevitably make, that come to them as striking contrasts, while other discriminations can be made only with difficulty or not at all. In between are the many discriminations that people can make readily but that they don't bother to make if there has never been a reason to pay attention to them or to develop skill in making them.

What we are learning about color categories is instructive. It seems that all humans, regardless of cultural differences, are inclined to make certain "basic" color discriminations, whether or not they have words in their language to reflect these discriminations. With color vocabulary, moreover, there is a definite order of elaboration of the discriminations for which there are distinct names (Berlin and Kay, 1969). The most basic distinction is between black and white (or dark and light); red is next added, then green and yellow (their order doesn't matter), then blue, followed by brown, and finally (in any order) purple, pink, orange, and grey.[27] Furthermore, whether red is the only verbalized category other than black and white or one of several, the focal point of reference on a color chart for what is most truly red remains fairly constant cross-culturally and cross-linguistically. This cross-cultural constancy of focal point obtains for other color terms as well. What varies is the range away from the focal point embraced by a color term.

As the study of color categories also shows, people do not represent in the vocabulary of their language all of the discriminations that they are able to make or that they actually do make. There are many familiar things in the environment of every one of us, for example, things that we recognize immediately upon encountering them and, in some cases, with which we have various associated feelings but for which we have no names. Wild flowers are an obvious example—things

---

[27]For a refinement of this sequence and its interpretation, see Witkowski and Brown (1977).

for which most urban Americans have no specific names and that they lump together under the broad label "flower," although they recognize differences among them. We refine the named categories of what we perceive insofar as it serves our interests to do so. Similarly with people, we learn the individual names of persons who are important to us and remember them for as long as these people continue to be important to us in some way. Others we do not catalogue separately and individually; we lump them together under broader class, ethnic, regional, national, and racial labels.

A language, then, provides a set of forms that is a code for other cultural forms. By representing the very large number of forms that we are able to discern by a more limited number of words in our language, we reduce the perceived forms in our experience to a small number of broader and more abstract coded categories (as we perceive more colors than we have words for). The words and stock phrases we use denote far fewer than the total range of forms we can discern and even talk about; but the formal categories they designate serve as the fixed points (or bands) of reference in the catalogue of forms with which we operate.

Our repeated use of these words allows us to approach a consensus regarding the range of forms they can denote. Such is not the case with forms we have come to discern in the course of our individual experiences but that we have no ready way to talk about. These tend to remain entities in our private, subjective worlds, entities that in some cases may be very important in our emotional lives, as psychiatric analysis reveals, but that we have great difficulty objectifying to ourselves.[28]

Many of the forms that are coded into a language's vocabulary can be described or defined by other words in that same vocabulary. The definition of these forms can therefore be derived from other forms that in a logical or systematic sense are more fundamental or primitive.

---

[28]The experiences of early childhood play an important role in psychotherapy presumably because they date from a time when language learning is as yet incomplete and people are not yet able to objectify these experiences to themselves and thereby to deal with them rationally.

But some forms represented in a vocabulary cannot be so defined. The distinctive features by which they are distinguished can be indicated only by demonstration. Once these primitive forms have been defined by example, the other forms can be defined in terms of various combinations of the primitive forms, as represented in verbal manipulation. A systematic description of a culture would properly begin with these primitive forms and then use them as the points of reference for describing the more complex forms derived from their various combinations. This approach is what anthropologists have in mind when they speak of describing a culture "in its own terms" and of emic ethnography.

The logic of description, however, does not recapitulate the ontogeny of learning. A descriptive grammar of a language, for example, one that develops its account step by step as logically as possible, does not present the steps by which people who learn the language in childhood arrive at an understanding of its grammar. We ordinarily learn a culture's forms gradually, through a series of successive phases and refinements of understanding, in the course of observing what people respond to selectively, both verbally and nonverbally. The vocabulary of their language, of course, provides a ready-made list of differentiated responses. To learn the language—that is, to learn to use its vocabulary acceptably—is indispensable for learning the cultural forms its vocabulary encodes. For this reason, anthropologists emphasize the importance of learning the local language in ethnographic study. Learning the language is not the only means for learning cultural forms, of course. Attention to nonverbal behavior is essential as well. But because of the importance of language for learning the forms in a culture, descriptive semantics is playing an increasingly important role in cultural description.[29]

Semantic studies reveal that the cultural forms designated by words have a systematic organization by virtue of the ways in which they

---

[29] A good selection of readings on developments in this area is provided by Tyler (1969). See also Burling (1970), Hammel (1965), and Buchler and Selby (1968).

contrast with one another. When we speak of red, blue, and brown, for example, we refer to perceptual categories that stand in immediate contrast with one another. Together with all other categories that also stand in immediate contrast with them, they constitute a **semantic domain**, in this case the domain designated by the word *color*. The perceptual categories represented by the words *sweet* and *sour* contrast directly with each other within the domain we call *taste*, but they do not contrast directly with *red* and *blue*. In answer to the question "Is it red?" one does not answer "No, it is sour." But the two domains we designate as *color* and *taste* do contrast directly at a more general level as broader categories of sensory experience. The conceptual forms represented by *father* and *uncle* similarly belong to a domain of kin relationships. They are not in direct contrast with the categories designated by *friend* and *enemy*, but they are subsumed with the latter at a higher level as parts of a larger domain of social relationships. As these examples show, some domains are designated by specific cover terms, such as *color* and *taste*, whereas others are not. We have no word in English for the domain of which the categories we call *enemy* and *friend* are immediate constituents. Semantic and allied forms of analysis allow us to sort the words people use and the cultural forms they designate according to their respective domains and subdomains. In this way the contrastive hierarchies into which they are ordered stand revealed. These hierarchies resemble the taxonomic hierarchies of biology, which are themselves self-consciously created examples of the kind of formal order we have been talking about. This kind of order seems to be present in the formal content of all cultures.

Such hierarchical or taxonomic orders are in part explicit and in part implicit in the patterns of contrast among the forms for which there are words and expressions. Such ordering of cultural forms is not always even implicit in the patterns of contrast revealed by semantic analysis of verbal behavior, but stands revealed by similar analysis of nonverbal behavior (Berlin, Breedlove, and Raven, 1968).

Semantic analysis reveals other patterns of organization in addition to hierarchical ones. They are discussed in the works already mentioned in footnote 29 and need not detain us further.

PROPOSITIONS

We not only discern forms, we discern various relations among forms: space relations, temporal relations, semantic and symbolic relations, relations of inclusion, exclusion, and complementarity, instrumental relations, and so on. Controversies over the measurement of individual capacities to perceive relationships by intelligence tests are of no concern to us here. What interests us is the use of language forms to designate the different categories of relation that people do learn to discern. The kinds of relations designated appear to be strikingly similar from language to language, however different the lexical or grammatical devices employed. This similarity is a major reason for our ability to translate from one language into another. It suggests much about the psychological and biological "constants" characterizing Homo sapiens as a species.

The encoding of relations as well as of forms in language allows us to use language to express, and thereby to objectify to ourselves, the relations we discern among forms. In other words, it allows us to state propositions, such as A is a kind of B, X is touching Z, etc. Some propositions are based on our experience of relations; others are not. For the capacity to formulate propositions allows us to reason by analogy. By substituting one coded category for another in various propositions, we can imagine new arrangements of forms by analogy with old ones, arrangements that we have not experienced directly at all, as when we go from the experiences of purple flowers and purple hats to the imagined experience of purple cows. Thus we arrive at a conception of new forms that we have not perceived but have constructed out of the verbal manipulations of already coded forms. These constructed forms or mental constructs may turn out to have some counterpart in later experience—indeed they may influence later experience—or, like ghosts and the ether of nineteenth-century physics, they may remain things whose existence we postulate but never directly observe.

Just such manipulation of propositions allows us to anticipate the future, that is, to describe events that have not yet occurred and that belong to fantasy. We cannot formulate purposes and goals except as we anticipate the future, and we cannot anticipate very far except as we are able to imagine things. The processes of linguistic codification and verbal manipulation that enable us to define complicated and long-range purposes also lead us to fill our world with products of our imagination. This power, provided by language as an objectifying codifier of experience and at the same time as a calculus for manipulating it imaginatively, is the prime factor responsible for the complexity and power of human knowledge—the phenomenon that so intrigued theorists of cultural evolution in the nineteenth century. As science fiction has demonstrated, what we imagine today we often realize tomorrow.

The human capacity to imagine—and, through imagination, to conjure up the future and make plans regarding it—produces a need to evaluate what is imagined in regard to the possibility or likelihood of its realization. Such evaluation takes two forms. One assesses the reasoning process—the logic—by which the imagined inference has been drawn. The other assesses the consistency of the inference with past experience. All people make both kinds of assessments, regardless of individual differences in the facility with which they make them. The experience of anthropologists leads to no other conclusion. All people, therefore, have standards of logic of some kind (whether or not they have made them an object of conscious attention), and they also have empirical standards for assessing the validity of propositions.

The extent to which these standards differ cross-culturally has not been investigated. Anthropologists who have learned the local language well enough to use it with some facility and who have discovered the propositions that are locally accepted as axiomatic, report that the way other people reason and points at which they catch one another out in argument seem reasonable to them. Consider, for example, the following comment by a Micronesian navigator, defending his belief that the sun goes around the earth (Girschner, 1913, p. 173, my translation).

> I am well aware of the foreigner's claim that the earth moves and the sun stands still, as someone once told us; but this we cannot believe, for how else could it happen that in the morning and evening the sun burns less hot than in the day? It must be because the sun has been cooled when it emerges from the water and toward setting it again approaches the water. And furthermore, how can it be possible that the sun remains still when we are yet able to observe that in the course of the year it changes its position in relation to the stars?

BELIEFS

The foregoing considerations lead us from propositions to beliefs, that is, to propositions that are accepted as true. Such acceptance, however, is not based on logical and empirical considerations alone. The fact that people hold what we regard as bizarre beliefs for reasons that we find empirically and logically unacceptable does not mean that they are therefore "prelogical" or "childlike" in mentality. To accept a proposition as true is simply to value it in some way. It may be valued on logical and empirical grounds or it may be valued for a variety of social and emotional reasons. Thus a belief may be held in spite of empirical evidence to the contrary for reasons that have nothing to do with its predictive utility. We need look no farther than the circle of our own family and friends for evidence of this.

Even logical and empirical consistency has its emotional side, as if some kind of rationality "drive" impels people to seek consistency. For when experience leads people to accept as true propositions that seem inconsistent with what they already believe, they are disturbed. Whatever the reasons may be, people seem compelled to try to resolve in some way the resulting cognitive dissonance, as psychologists call it (Festinger, 1957). Basically the technique of resolution is to postulate an additional proposition that, if true, would account for the apparent contradictions. For example, if someone tells us something contrary to our beliefs, we assume that he is lying or is misinformed. When we have experienced something that doesn't fit our beliefs, we may assume that it was an illusion. A common assumption is that the contradictory propositions pertain to different domains of reality and are not therefore mutually contradictory. Thus many people in Truk have decided that there are two kinds of illness, a general kind for which western medicine is effective and a local Trukese kind that requires resort to traditional Trukese medicine.

The more people segregate their experiences into independent domains, the greater the corresponding number of strategies for action they must develop. The wider the range of situations for which a strategy seems applicable, the easier it becomes to deal with day-to-day problems. A postulate that joins otherwise separate domains of experience, making it possible to understand all of them in the same terms, is very appealing. Making such postulates is, of course, what the construction of scientific theory is all about. But it is also a feature of the human intellectual process everywhere.

The construction of postulates that rationalize experience, clearing up inconsistencies in it and uniting domains into broader categories, is essential for complex learning to take place. By construing many isolated facts as following from one principle, people are freed to handle more facts. When we know the "principle of the thing," we become masters of a large body of otherwise disparate things, and a single overall strategy becomes applicable to a wide range of phenomena. As a consequence of human rationalizing of this sort, beliefs tend to be ordered into coherent and internally consistent systems. Some of the specific beliefs in these systems are rooted in daily experience and appear to be self-evident truths. Others are inferences drawn from them and logically consistent with them. Still others are postulates that integrate the self-evident truths and inferred truths in that they all seem to follow logically from the postulates. Such other propositions as follow logically from the unifying postulates are also plausible truths.

Consider as an illustration the common human experience that unpleasant things happen to us when our actions have offended our fellows and that a display of contrition and atonement predisposes them to us favorably again. These observations and the propositions following from them provide a strategy for mitigating the punishments we might otherwise have to endure. We suffer many other unpleasantnesses as well, often for no reason we can readily perceive. If we postulate the existence of unseen beings that are easily offended, we can then understand misfortune generally as punishment for offenses we have given to others, and we can extend our strategy of contrition and atonement as a technique for handling all kinds of misfortune. We are inclined to accept such unifying postulates as true because they seem to make so many things clear. We are reluctant to question their truth because of the cognitive disorder and operational uncertainty that would seem to follow from our disbelief.

Other things also predispose people to particular beliefs. The greater experience and wisdom of elders, where conditions of life are relatively stable, gives authority and credibility to the beliefs they express. All too often, to go against their advice is to end in failure. Some beliefs are self-validating in that, believing something to be true, people act in such a way as to make their future experience consistent with their beliefs. The paranoid, for example, who believes people are hostile, acts on this belief in such a way as to invite their hostility. Beliefs about human character and motives and about sorcery and witchcraft often work in such self-validating ways. Propositions that provide emotional gratification also invite belief. Many religious beliefs function in this manner, as also do beliefs about people and their nature. If, for example, we say on the one hand that all people, as human beings, are entitled to certain considerations, and if, at the same time, we refuse to show these considerations to some particular category of persons, we face the problem of being guilty of violating our own principles. But if we believe that those whose humanity we dishonor in our conduct are, after all, not fully human, "still hardly out of the trees," or the like, then we can ease our consciences. To believe otherwise is to be confronted with our guilt.

The emotional factors that commit men to the truth of particular propositions take us into the realm of values, to be discussed below. But one thing requires mention. The emotional bases for commitment to any proposition obviously vary from individual to individual. With some propositions, emotional factors may be widely shared because of common problems arising from common experience, such as the problem of guilt referred to above. But with other propositions, their emotional value may be highly varied, so that they are strongly held by some and mean little to others. Important for a sense of community, however, is the human tendency to systematize beliefs in the course of rationalizing experience, so that in all cultures beliefs tend to be ordered into systems. Individuals may vary greatly in their personal commitment to the truth of individual propositions within a system of beliefs and yet share a common commitment to the system as such and to its master propositions.

So far we have concentrated on considerations that lead a person to accept a proposition as true without regard to the beliefs of others. Obviously we must distinguish between a proposition that a person is privately convinced is true and one that he acts on as if it were true.

We may refuse to eat tomatoes, for example, saying that they are poisonous (as our recent European forebears seemed to believe) without being at all convinced that they really are so. Or we may, when ill, take a medicine dutifully as prescribed, although we privately doubt that it really makes any difference, just as we may pray for rain with little expectation that it will do any good. Often we act as if we hold certain propositions to be true because we think that others believe them and expect us to act accordingly. There are times, of course, when a strongly held private conviction will lead us to act in a manner that is contrary to the expectations of our fellows and counter to what we know they believe. But what is important for coordinated social interaction and mutual understanding is not necessarily a common personal commitment to the truth of a particular set of propositions—although such a common commitment may be essential for cooperation in some kinds of endeavor—but a knowledge by all parties of the propositions on which actions are predicated and a common acceptance of these propositions as a basis for action. When we cite propositions in justification for our acts, we are treating them as if they are true, regardless of our private convictions.

We must distinguish, therefore, between **private beliefs**, propositions that a person accepts as true irrespective of the beliefs of others, and **declared beliefs,** propositions a person gives the appearance of accepting as true in his public behavior and speech and that he cites in argument or to justify his actions to others. The propositions that a group's members agree to accept as their common declared beliefs are the group's **public beliefs.** Wallace (1961, p. 41) has observed that if "any set of individuals establish a system of equivalent behavioral expectancies, an organized relationship comes into existence. Such a system of mutual expectancies may be termed an *implicit contract* .... Culture can be conceived as a set of standardized models of such contractual relationships." Parents and children, for example, need not privately believe the same things about Santa Claus to enjoy Christmas together, but they must have workably equivalent understandings of what are the public beliefs with which the game of Christmas is to be played and of what must be done to give them the semblance of truth. (For a fuller discussion of beliefs and belief systems, see Black, 1973.)

VALUES

In human experience every form is associated in some way with other forms. All the objects, persons, practices, and events in a person's conceptual repertory of forms have in this respect some kind of associational or symbolic meaning for him. Our concern here is with the ways people associate things with their inner feeling states and with the gratification of their wants and felt needs,[30] in other words, with how people value things.

As we know, people do not simply value some things positively and other things negatively. The same objects can both gratify and pain us. The persons who are the principal agents of our gratifications are likely also to be the principal agents of our frustrations—as parents are likely to be to their children. Our feelings about things are therefore ambivalent and full of conflicts. How to handle these conflicts—resolve them if we can, live with them if we must—is a major human concern. People deal with them by resorting to such psychological mechanisms as displacement, projection, sublimation, and reaction formation, which may lead to beliefs that seem bizarre and give rise to customs from which it is difficult to see how people derive any gratification whatsoever, such as painful and medically dangerous rites. (These are discussed at some length by Whiting and Child, 1953, and by W. Goodenough, 1963, Chapter 6. See also Levine, 1973.)

The pattern of recurring gratifications and frustrations in relation to the things around us is inevitably unique for each of us. Everyone, therefore, has his own personal sentiment system: the preferences that would guide his actions if he felt free of all social restraint. And everyone has a corresponding private or personal set of value attitudes toward things. The more similar the conditions under which people grow up, the more similar in a general way their private values are likely to be, though still differing greatly in detail. People will have experienced much the same

---

[30] "By wants . . . we refer to desired states of affairs, and by needs, we refer to effective means for achieving or maintaining them" (W. Goodenough, 1963, p. 50). Compare Malinowski (1944, p. 90), who defines needs as the sufficient and necessary conditions for group survival rather than as the sufficient conditions for accomplishing desired ends (including group survival when it is a desired end).

things in similar ways. They may end up ranking them differently in their preference hierarchies, but there will be a number of things that they all view positively and a number of other things that they all find repellent. The sense that other people have sentiments and private values similar to our own—in that we are positively and negatively oriented in similar directions—gives us a feeling that we and they are of one kind. When we see others choosing as we would choose under similar circumstances, we feel that we understand them. We may even feel that there is a special bond between us. Such feelings are a major contributor to social solidarity, the kind of solidarity that the French sociologist Emile Durkheim called "mechanical" by contrast with "organic solidarity," which is based on mutual dependence for the gratification of wants and not on the sharing of common interests and sentiments.

Human experience, both actual and imaginary, is richly diversified. Along with this diversification goes a diversification of wants and interests. They cannot possibly all be satisfied. Rather, they often conflict and compete with one another. How to maximize gratification and minimize frustration becomes a major human concern. This concern leads not only to the ordering of wants and interests into preference hierarchies; it also leads to an organization of resources for want gratification and to an organization of human activity with respect to their use. People maximize the gratification of their wants by scheduling, and they minimize the chances of frustration by stockpiling resources and husbanding their consumption.

A New Guinea villager, for example, knows that he can allow only so much time to elapse between garden plantings if he is to have a continuous supply of vegetable food. He knows how much additional food he will have to provide in order to sponsor a memorial festival in honor of his dead father, for which he will have to plan five or six years ahead. He budgets his time in hunting, housebuilding, trading, and warring with his neighbors accordingly.

Such budgeting is possible only within a framework of established schedules and their consequent routines. Scheduling orders the conduct of much that goes on in every human community. The kinds of activities in which people spend much of their time and the circumstances in which they conduct them make a difference, to be sure, in the degree to which scheduling and routinization are rewarding. Human communities vary greatly in this respect. Nevertheless, the tendency to schedule and to routinize, insofar as it is rewarding to do so, is universal. Even the recluse orders his life in terms of fixed routines.

Because schedules and routines provide for the gratification of otherwise mutually incompatible wants, they are themselves a source of gratification. They acquire further positive value by reducing uncertainty about gratification and increasing the reliability of expectations. They relieve people of having to make sometimes difficult decisions about what to do when, and they help to space activities so as to maximize their combined, overall efficacy. Insofar as they provide these kinds of gratification, people will value positively the established schedules and routines within which they customarily operate.

RULES AND PUBLIC VALUES

Just as schedules are needed to regulate and thereby maximize the gratification of competing wants within each individual, they are also needed to regulate competition and mutual interference among different individuals as they all simultaneously seek to accomplish their respective purposes. When they do not get in one another's way, there is no problem; but for a great many of their most important wants people are dependent on the cooperation of others to achieve them. Often a person can get what he wants only at someone else's expense. Each of us feels a need, therefore, to restrict and control the behavior of others and at the same time to remain as free as possible from restriction and control by them.

The resolution of these common competing interests is to schedule the gratification of wants through social rules or codes of conduct. These rules govern how certain categories of persons may act in relation to various other categories of persons and things. The rules, in other words, specify how rights and privileges in persons and things are to be socially distributed. American children are first introduced to this kind of interpersonal scheduling as "taking turns." Anthropologists know of no human community that is without such rules or whose social relationships cannot be analyzed as an ordered distribution of rights, privileges, and duties among well-defined categories of persons. In this respect, the conduct of human affairs everywhere is ordered with reference to a "social contract" of some kind, if we may borrow the term that has become so firmly associated with the political philosophies of Hobbes, Locke, and Rousseau (for discussion, see Kendall, 1968).

Right, privilege, and **duty** are indeed fundamental etic concepts for studying the culture of social relationships.[31] They are technically used by anthropologists according to the definition given them by the legal theorist Wesley Hohfeld (1919). In the relations between two parties A and B, what A can demand of B (under the rules) is A's right or demand right of B and is correspondingly B's duty to A. What A cannot demand of B (A's nonright) is correspondingly B's privilege or privilege right. (The term privilege is often used popularly in another sense to mean a right accorded by an authority that is empowered to make or change the rules, as distinct from a "god-given," "natural," or "inalienable" right, which such authority itself has the duty of honoring, as when people argue as to whether the vote is a "right" or a "privilege.") Rights and duties define both the limitations on behavior and the priorities among persons in relation to the gratification of wants. Within the boundaries thus delimited is the range of privilege. Here people are free, according to the rules, to do what they wish without regard to the wishes of others. A system of social rules is basically, then, a definition of rights and corresponding duties.

The pattern of priorities expressed in a body of social rules represents a set of values. Insofar as people are willing to govern their conduct in accordance with these rules, they demonstrate their acceptance of these values, at least in public. The values expressed by a given set of rules are thus the **operating values** of those who abide by them; and they are the **public values** of any social group whose members regard observing these rules as a condition of membership in the group. One individual may belong to several groups, each with its own rules and corresponding public values, as with an American who is an active member of the Methodist Church, the local country club, and the National Guard.

---

[31] For a discussion of their use as analytical tools, see W. Goodenough (1965) and Keesing (1970b).

Whatever one of these value systems he selects as his operating values
of the moment depends on the group that is serving as his reference
group.

A group's public values reflect in many ways the personal sentiments
and values of its members. But they are bound to conflict with personal
preferences, at least in part. People often violate the rules or seek to
subvert them. But we should not conclude that the demands a system
of rules makes on an individual contrary to his private preferences
necessarily lead him to want to do away with the rules. They may be
inconvenient on some occasions, but the same rules may be to his
advantage on others. For example, the inconvenience a man must suffer
in Truk in Micronesia because of the authority over him his wife's
brother enjoys under the rules is matched by the same authority he
enjoys over his sister's husband.[32] To change the rules to escape their
onus is also to remove a source of advantage. Moreover, although the
rules force us to give the other fellow his due, they protect us from
being otherwise frustrated by our fellows in pursuing our own interests.
The rules and the public values they express are themselves valued as
something to which appeal can be made. The frustration a person
suffers from their operation enables him to demonstrate his endorse-
ment of them and gives him a righteous claim to exercise the privileges
they allow him and to demand that others acquiesce. Thus the system
of rules gives to every man a hold on his fellows, something he cannot
afford to lose even though it may cost him much.

However, no system of rules that has ever been devised accords to
every category of person the same rights and duties in relation to every
other category. Everywhere the possession of at least some rights and
privileges is contingent upon meeting qualifications of some kind.
There are natural differences in age, sex and reproductive role, tempera-
ment, and intellectual aptitudes. Together with concomitant differences in skill, knowledge, experience, and wisdom, they are enough to
guarantee inequalities in mutual dependency and in real power to implement or interfere with the gratification of one another's wants. Such

---

[32] For an ethnographic study of public values in Truk, see Caughey (1977).

inequalities tend to become magnified in societies where occupational and other specialization is highly developed or where other factors also serve to promote complicated patterns of mutual dependence. The inequalities of real power to which these complexities are conducive tend to find expression in the social rules, whose shape is inevitably influenced more heavily by the interests of those who enjoy the greater real power. It follows that in some societies some categories of person enjoy far fewer rights and privileges than other categories enjoy in the aggregate of relationships in which they operate. Persons who are thus most "deprived" by the rules have less incentive to honor them. As their circumstances change, moreover, people gain or lose advantages under the rules. There is, therefore, continual pressure from individuals and groups within a society to modify the rules, as Tanner (1970) has shown in her study of legal process among the Minangkabau of Sumatra. People may agree on the content of existing rules, but they are unlikely to be equally committed to keeping that content in its present form or to accepting the public values it expresses. In their efforts to bend the rules to conflicting ends, they may even choose to disagree regarding their present content.

People have to teach their children the rules. They also justify their own actions to one another by reference to the rules and to the public values they understand the rules to embody. But we cannot expect their formulations always to match closely the way they respond to specific situations, even when they consider their response to be in conformity with the rules. Popular formulations are often approximations, at best, of what closer analysis reveals the rules apparently to be. In the study of unwritten law, for example, it is necessary to analyze a sizable body of case materials—with special attention to the exceptional cases—in order to learn the things people actually take into account when they decide whether a given action in a given situation is a violation of another's rights. Ordinary verbalizations of the rules tend to put them in general terms, leaving out the additional considerations that complicate them. The same problems occur here as occur when people try to describe the grammatical rules of a language.

Close and careful analysis of the rules is required to get at the values they express. Proverbs, myths, stories, and fables also provide evidence of public values and of their fit or lack of it with private sentiments.

For example, when people enjoy telling stories about trickster heroes whose actions are outrageous according to their rules of conduct, they are often giving expression, among other things, to their private feelings about the rules.

The ambivalence of people toward their society's rules is in part responsible for the special feelings that we associate with morality. Because under the rules we must suffer many of our wants to be frustrated at the hands of our fellows, we have strong emotional feelings about our rights and privileges. What a system of rules does, in effect, is to define for each of us the limits of our frustration. Within these limits we are free to seek what gratifications we can find and even, on occasion, to demand them. All of the anger that is the natural response to frustration and that we often have had to suppress in connection with the demands others rightfully can make upon us—all of this suppressed anger can be released as righteous wrath when our rights are violated. Our wrath has a special quality arising from a sense of betrayal. Because the rules are the basis for expectations people have of one another, people count on their being honored. To present oneself as a member of a community or other social group is to pledge oneself to honor its rules. Not to honor them is to betray a trust. Because the rules frustrate as well as reward us, our commitment to abide by them is in some ways a sacrifice in which we give something up in return for something else. Insofar as our fellows fail to make the same commitment, we lose what our own commitment was supposed to give us. We are tempted, therefore, to break the rules ourselves when we see others break them. We are thus placed in emotional conflict. Our recommitment to the rules is likely to be accompanied by a desire for strong punitive sanction against whoever transgressed, even when we were not ourselves wronged.

For such reasons the strong emotions of righteousness and outrage naturally accompany commitment to a body of social rules. The presence of these emotions makes the difference between what Sumner (1907) long ago distinguished as "folkways" and "mores." If all human societies are ordered by rules specifying rights and duties, we need not wonder that these emotions and the peculiar affective tone we associate with "morality" and "right and wrong" should be universal human phenomena. Every social order necessarily contains within it a moral order. (For further discussion in the context of social evolution, see W. Goodenough, 1967.)

RECIPES

Forms, beliefs, and values are the points of reference for behavior. An actor perceives a situation (including the behavior of others) as an arrangement or sequence of interpretable forms. The values he attaches to these forms and his beliefs about their interrelations allow him to relate them to his own internal feeling states. They help him to diagnose the causes of his discontents and to specify his wants. His beliefs about them provide the basis for determining what rearrangements of forms within his situation will satisfy his wants. He must take account of established schedules and social rules in deciding on a course of action that, according to his beliefs, is calculated to achieve the necessary rearrangements. A break with schedule and a breach of the rules may appear to be the only course possible, in which case he must weigh the possible cost of such action against the cost of leaving the particular wants unmet.

To say all this does not mean that human action succeeds in optimizing gratifications. We all miscalculate a good deal of the time. Wants that we conceal from ourselves often lead us to act in ways we later regret. The point remains that human behavior is directed toward accomplishing purposes, whether simple or complicated. As such, it is means-ends oriented and calculated with reference to utilitarian considerations of some kind, the ultimate measure of utility being a person's internal feeling states—emotional as well as physical—and not what an observer estimates his overall best interests to be.

Purposes and goals, then, are what give coherence to action; and it is in terms of the purposes and goals we understand others to have (or that we impute to them) that we make sense of their actions. All meaningful behavior is in this respect like speech behavior. The communicational intent of an utterance provides the focus around which words and grammatical constructions are selected and arranged syntactically into coherent sentences. Similarly, the intended consequences or purposes of other kinds of behavior provide the foci around which people, things, and acts become organized syntactically into coherent activities. Indeed, an activity may be defined as any action or coordinated grouping of actions that is aimed at affecting in some way existing arrangements, as these are defined by some set of cultural forms. The arrangements may be material, social, or emotional; and the intended rearrangements may be valued as ends in themselves or be seen as needed to realize some more distant purpose.

Accomplishing some purposes is an *ad hoc* affair in which people improvise as they go along, making do with whatever resources are at hand. This is inevitable when people face problems for which they have no prior solutions; but it is also frequent with simple purposes that are easily met in a wide variety of ways. Even in such *ad hoc* activities, however, what things are done and the order in which they are done are governed by the actors' beliefs about the elements involved and by the actors' existing skills and behavioral habits. These beliefs, skills, and habits impose constraints on the conduct of an activity even when people are improvising. There may be considerable room for variation within these constraints. Nevertheless, there are almost always some constraints of this kind, and they give an overall structure to the conduct of activities, providing them with their basic syntactic organization. Social rules of conduct, of course, add more constraints, prescribing and proscribing the kinds of things that may be said and done and the order of their occurrence.

The constraints on behavior, whether imposed by nature and circumstances or by beliefs, skills, habits, and rules, complicate the improvisation of activity, making it difficult. For most recurring purposes, therefore, people develop recipes or formulas. These reduce the amount of improvisation needed but at the same time add even more constraints, further structuring the syntactic organization of human activity.

Every recipe, indeed, is a statement of a set of conditions that must be fulfilled if an objective is to be met. There are requirements as to raw materials, tools, skills, time, space, and personnel; and there are requirements as to how these are to be organized or effectively related to one another. In some recipes the requirements are very precise, allowing for little variation, whereas in others there is a wide range of latitude possible once the requirements have been met. For example, a task may require a minimum of two men to execute, but be more effectively carried out with three, four, or five men. For some purposes, again, only oak wood will suffice, but for others any hardwood will do. The ordering of forms into taxonomic hierarchies, to which we referred earlier, represents a practical cognitive adaptation to the way degrees of specificity vary among different recipes.

The purposes for which recipes are designed are not confined to material things. Many of our recurring purposes have to do with people: persuading someone to do us a favor, getting permission for something we are not at liberty to do on our own, and so on. These recipes pertain to comportment: the ways in which we should dress, the ways in which we should approach others, the things we should and should not say to them. Emily Post and Dale Carnegie are well-known authors of recipe books for purposes of this kind in the United States. All peoples have recipes for staging parties, for wooing the opposite sex, for making friends, and for making enemies. Berne (1964) gives many examples of the standard recipes used by Americans in what he calls the "games people play."

Some recipes have been thought through in advance, being deduced from existing beliefs and understandings. Others are arrived at through trial and error; procedures are found that seem to work, but why they work is not understood. When we think we understand the principles involved, we feel free to vary a recipe in accordance with our understanding; but when we do not understand the principles, we tend to adhere slavishly to the formula, hoping each time that it will continue to work as it has on occasion in the past. If we have little at stake, we can afford to experiment with it so as to improve our understanding; but if our concern about the outcome is high, we try to follow the recipe exactly. Indeed, behavior tends to acquire a slavish or compulsive quality, and in this sense to become ritualized, in connection with recurring purposes that are of high emotional concern to us (whatever the reasons for the concern may be), especially when we are not confident of our understanding of all that is involved.[33]

---

[33]Malinowski (1925) has argued, for example, that magical rites and spells tend to be used most intensively at those points in technological procedures where human control of the outcome is least certain. For further discussion see W. Goodenough (1963, pp. 477-478).

Because it is often difficult to meet the requirements of a particular recipe, people are interested in opportunities to learn new ones for accomplishing the same or similar purposes. Regardless of how frequently they resort to them, they feel more secure if they have knowledge of alternative recipes (or have access to the services of people with such knowledge). For example, to have fish to go with a cooked starch food at the main meal of the day is a serious concern of many Pacific Islanders. In any one locality, people know a number of different ways to catch fish. Each method or recipe has its own requirements for equipment, skills, and personnel. Each is productive under some conditions and for some kinds of fish. There are occasions when circumstances offer little choice of method, and there are others when several possibilities are open. Moreover, the people prefer some over others as being less arduous, more exciting or challenging, potentially more productive, or socially more fun, interests that are often in competition with one another. Such multiple, competing interests motivate local retention of a larger repertory of fishing methods (recipes) than would be dictated by considerations of productive efficiency alone. People switch from one method to another in accordance with their interests of the moment and as circumstances permit.

As the example of fishing reminds us, people have many different interests and they try to serve as many as they can simultaneously through the same activities. To go fishing can help meet dietary, recreational, and other purposes all at once. To the extent that any one recipe allows for variation in how it can be executed, people can adapt it to achieving other purposes as well. What evolves as the established way of conducting a recurring activity, therefore, is likely to have been shaped with reference to several different interests and purposes at once.

ROUTINES AND CUSTOMS

We have deliberately talked about recipes rather than about routines and customs. The understanding or knowledge of procedural requirements for accomplishing a purpose—that is, a recipe—should not be confused with the manner in which the requirements tend to be met in practice or with the regularity with which resort is made to a particular recipe among several known alternatives. These things are not unrelated, to be sure; but when we speak of recipes, we refer to ideas and understandings about how to do things, and when we speak of routines and customs, we refer to the actual doing of them.

Within the latitude a recipe allows, people develop personal procedural habits and personal styles of operation, thereby routinizing their execution of the recipe. The recipe for setting the table for dinner, for example, calls for a tablecloth, for certain kinds of dishes, glassware, and silverware, and for arranging them in a certain way. Physical necessity requires that the tablecloth be put on first, but the recipe says nothing about the order in which things are to be done otherwise. Each of us, however, tends to develop his own habitual routine for the order in which he sets out the dishes, silverware, and glassware.

Routines of this kind may remain personal idiosyncrasies; but in activities calling for cooperative participation by several people, the personal style of a dominant individual may determine the manner in which a particular recipe is carried out by all. Repeated performances by the same persons will result in a set of mutual expectations and mutually adjusted habits that may be shaped largely by the individual style of one of them. This is especially likely in a teaching situation where children learn from participation with adults. The resulting expectations become, in effect, a part of the recipe—the right way to do it—for the activity in question in the thinking of people who continually work together. If a person works with different groups of others in the same activity, he will perceive the several groups' different expectations as variant ways of executing the same basic recipe; but if he works only with the same group of others, he may incorporate their expectations as to manner of execution into his conception of the recipe itself. There is thus a feedback relationship between recipes and the behavioral routines for executing them.

People who work with one another in a number of different activities, following different recipes, are likely to carry their mutually adjusted habits in one activity over to the others, insofar as the recipes allow it. Their mutual expectations thus become generalized, giving an overall style to the way many different things are done. As these expectations are fed back into the recipes, they too become a part of the standards for doing a variety of different things. The several recipes to which these generalized standards apply now constitute a distinct class of recipes with a more highly structured syntactic organization than is needed for any one of them on technical grounds alone. Such developments are evident in the social organization of work, for example, where the same expectations for giving orders, initiating work, coordinating effort, allocating tasks and responsibilities, remunerating labor, and expressing approval and disapproval carry over from activity to activity.

Unlike routines, which arise from habits of executing particular recipes, customs have to do with habits of choice among alternative recipes and alternative developed routines. When people have to get together and discuss which among alternative recipes or known routines they will use on a given occasion, no one of the recipes or routines can be said to be the custom for the occasion. A custom, then, is a recipe or a routine for executing a recipe that is regularly resorted to, circumstances permitting, in preference to alternative recipes or alternative routines for executing them. Customs arise when the choice of recipes or routines for given occasions has itself been routinized.

We should note that routinization may relate only to the choice of recipes and not to the manner of their execution. Thus there may be customary recipes for digging wells in a community where there is need to dig a well only once in a decade or so, and there may be established expectations as to which among these recipes will be used under given conditions; but it is unlikely that there will be established routines for performing these recipes, given the infrequency with which wells are dug. By contrast, the customary recipes for preparing staple foods, being executed frequently, are likely to be highly routinized. Behavioral routines are not likely to develop except in relation to the performance of customary recipes, but some customary recipes may lack such associated customary routines.

Some customary recipes are not used if circumstances permit the use of alternatives. Those that are preferred, circumstances permitting, are primary customs, whereas those that are habitually resorted to when circumstances do not allow for use of preferred recipes are secondary customs. The status of a recipe as customary does not depend on its being preferred as the "ideal" one to use, other things being equal, but on its being the one habitually used (and thus expected to be used) under a given set of conditions, including conditions that preclude resort to otherwise preferred recipes. It is important to note that people in two communities may have knowledge of much the same recipes but have different customs regarding their use.

Because customs are recipes and routines to which people regularly resort for recurring purposes, people become themselves adapted or habituated to them, and they become skilled in performing them. Customs thus acquire a value over and above that deriving from their efficacy in relation to the purposes they were designed to accomplish. People become committed to doing things to which they are habituated and that therefore "come naturally" to them. This commitment may lead them to demand of one another the use of particular recipes and routines as a part of their rules of conduct. When this happens, a custom reflects a social duty and not just habit alone. Here, again, we encounter a consideration in the distinction Sumner (1907) made between customs that are "mores" and those that are "folkways."

Once a custom has been established, the requirements for enacting it become a constraint affecting the form that other recipes and routines can readily take. The form of existing customs serves to limit the form of other customs and to limit what among known alternative recipes can readily become customary. The form of a custom cannot be understood, therefore, with reference only to the purposes it is intended to serve. It must also be interpreted in light of the other customs with which it coexists, its possible effects on them, and their possible effects on it. We are thus reminded, again, that a utilitarian interpretation of a custom must take account of its net efficacy with respect to all the other purposes that people also have and that they seek to implement through their other customs.

Obviously, some recurring purposes take priority over others. Recipes that are effective in accomplishing what people regard as their basic survival needs and their basic requirements of social living are more likely to become customary at the expense of other recipes for accomplishing other purposes, and the latter are less likely to become customary at the expense of the former. Other considerations also govern the relative ease and difficulty with which the forms of customary recipes can be mutually adapted. They include the extent to which recipes require social consensus, the investment in learning and skills that people have already made in them, and the kind and intensity of emotional investment people have in them. We do not yet know how much weight these considerations have relative to one another or how their respective weights change with circumstances. Theories regarding the primacy of technology and of material considerations over social and other human interests (for example, White, 1949) provide only a crude approximation of what seems to be a very complicated interplay of competing concerns. Men sometimes choose to die rather than to compromise beliefs or customary practices that have little to do with physical survival but to which, for other reasons, they are emotionally committed—an observation that reminds us how complicated the matter of priorities actually is.

SYSTEMS OF CUSTOMS

We have already seen how the development of skills and the need for mutuality of expectations, each in its own way, serve to commit people to particular recipes and routines rather than to known alternatives. Commitment seems to be involved in the process of what we ordinarily speak of as institutionalization, for we usually have in mind that a recipe or routine has become established as the expected thing to do and, with increasing degrees of institutionalization, the necessary and even morally proper thing to do. The mutual adjustment of customary recipes and routines to one another greatly reinforces commitment to them and, hence, their becoming institutionalized, for it leads to organized systems whose several component customs are so adjusted to one another as to make change in any one of them likely to disrupt the operation of all the others. The so-called chain effect of change has been well documented in many societies (see, for example, Spicer, 1952; Paul, 1955). An understanding of the systemic organization of customs can reveal much about the structure of institutions as well as about the process of social and cultural change.

We have seen that a customary recipe contains a variety of features, including such things as raw materials, tools, skills, specific operations, time and space requirements, personnel requirements, and occasions for performance. (For fuller listing and discussion, see W. Goodenough,

1963, pp. 324-331.) Different recipes stand in different relationships to one another, such as feature overlap (having some features in common), feature complementarity (having no features in common), and instrumental linkage (the purpose of one recipe being to prepare the materials or set the stage for use of another recipe).

Instrumental linkage clearly imposes constraints on the temporal ordering or scheduling of activities. Fully complementary recipes, on the other hand, can be conducted at the same time, since they involve no overlap of materials, skills, personnel, etc. When recipes have some features in common, however, there is also a need for their systematic ordering. The kinds of order possible become complicated by the several ways in which their features overlap. To the extent that two recipes require the same raw materials, skills, settings, and persons, they tend to be in competition. Scheduling, as we saw in connection with competing wants, is an obvious solution to this problem. The occasions for performing the recipes are thus made complementary. If one recipe permits of wider alternatives in raw materials, settings, and so on, than another, it may become customary to use for the former recipe those alternatives that cannot be used in the latter, thus making complementary what were overlapping recipes initially. It may also happen that two recipes have common procedural requirements such that a single performance of the common procedures will simultaneously promote the purposes of both. The interests of efficiency may make the performance of one such activity the occasion for regularly performing the other as well. If withdrawing money from the bank, shopping for food, and getting books from the library all require us to drive to town, for example, we are likely to combine the occasions for these several activities, letting one trip to town serve them all. Similarly, if the same work crew is needed to get several different kinds of jobs done, timing of its mobilization may be geared to occasions when there is need for more than one of them to be undertaken. The recipes for different recurring purposes are often adjusted, where flexibility is possible, to facilitate such fusions or partial fusions of what would otherwise be discrete activities.

Such fusions, as well as the instrumental and complementary relations of recipes, affect the development of customary schedules for the performance of activities. People try to arrange things so as to be able to engage in as many rewarding activities as possible at optimal intervals. Complementary arrangements of recipe features (as with the division of labor and skills) contribute importantly to this end, as does the use of feature overlaps to fuse the performance of activities into efficient customary routines.

There are, of course, limits to which the gearing of customary recipes together into schedules and fusions can go. Changing circumstances affect the availability of material resources, personnel, and skills and variously restrict or expand the possibilities for using particular recipes. The consequences can be disruptive of highly structured schedules. People need alternative recipes and alternative schedules in order to accomplish their purposes adaptively in an unstable world. But the time and energy needed to learn alternative procedures and to develop alternative skills diminish the time and energy available for other, more immediately gratifying activities. The more alternatives people must be prepared to take, the more difficult it is for them to arrange things socially and materially so as to perform any one of them easily and efficiently. By contrast, the more fully conditions allow people to follow one set of recipes and one schedule of activities, the freer they are to accumulate the necessary raw materials and tools, to develop the particular skills required, and to organize personnel into appropriate standing groups. To the extent that conditions allow, therefore, people commit themselves to particular recipes and schedules. And as we have seen, their subsequent greater familiarity with these recipes and schedules serves to reinforce this commitment even more.

The stronger this commitment, the less people remain concerned to keep themselves ready and able to resort to alternatives. They become increasingly concerned, instead, to arrange their world so that the need for alternatives will not arise. The recipes, stockpiles of materials, social arrangements, and schedules to which people commit themselves increasingly acquire value as ends in themselves. People demand of one another that they acquire the knowledge and skills needed to perform these routines. They demand cooperation of one another in their performance, and they prohibit behavior that interferes with them or that jeopardizes the arrangements and stockpiles on which performance of these customary routines depends, investing them with moral rightness and even sanctity. Thus the processes that lead to the gearing together of customs into complex organizations of human activity and social relationships provide human incentives to keep existing customs and arrangements capable of continued effective operation. The customary procedures and the standing arrangements to which such conservative commitment has been made by a community's members may be said to make up that community's **institutions**.[34]

Because they develop in the interest of increasing the efficiency with which valued ends can be readily achieved, institutions tend to crystallize around the points where recipe features overlap and where the conduct of activities can be readily fused. The organization of interpersonal dealings and the constitution of social groups are especially prone to being institutionalized. Mutuality of expectations is so essential to the conduct of all activities requiring cooperation among several individuals that people are under great pressure to reduce alternative modes of social organization to a minimum and, where alternatives exist, to commit themselves to one of them as the established way of doing business. For example, why have a different way of structuring leader-follower relations for each different activity if one will serve effectively for all? A community's standing groups, such as its families, clans, commercial and military companies, and other permanent associations, tend all to be internally ordered according to similar principles and similar patterns of role relationships. So much is this the case that we take it largely for granted. It would seem strange, indeed, to have a totally different language for every activity in which we engage and entirely different rules of conduct for every recipe calling for social cooperation. The recurring principles and patterns of organization and priority that link recipes and institutions together give them coherence and structural order in a larger system. These principles and patterns also give an individual character to such systems as wholes, the kind of quality that Ruth Benedict (1934) sought

---

[34]This definition is consistent with that of Talcott Parsons (1951, p. 39). Some writers use the term "institution" in a somewhat different sense. Thus "an institution is a group of people" according to Coon (1962, p. 3). See also Malinowski (1944, pp. 52-54), who used "institution" much in the sense of a customary recipe and its associated customary routine or routines.

to elucidate as "patterns of culture" and that Morris Opler (1945) discussed in terms of cultural "themes."

MEANING AND FUNCTION

We have talked of recipes as formulas for accomplishing purposes and gratifying wants. We have looked at the conflict of wants and at the consequent need for schedules and priorities. And we have considered how the human tendency to optimize the gratification of wants leads people to adjust their customary routines and schedules to one another in highly organized and institutionalized systems. In all this, we have been taking as axiomatic that human behavior is purposeful and that the consequences of past actions, relative to people's purposes, affect the ways people value things and the decisions they make regarding future actions. However they may be phrased, the same axioms clearly underlie utility theory in economics and learning theory in psychology. Concern with consequences and their effects on future behavior is also reflected in the concept of function, which has been developed in anthropology in two somewhat different senses by Malinowski (1944) and Radcliffe-Brown (1935).[35]

According to Malinowski, customs and institutions come into being in response to basic human needs—such as for food, sex, and shelter—and such other needs as may have derived from social living. To look at how customs and institutions satisfy these needs is to examine their function. In other words, Malinowski saw customs and institutions as functioning to solve the recurring problems of living.

Radcliffe-Brown and his followers took physiology as their model. Seeing society as like an organism whose several different parts contribute, each in its own way, to the continuing existence of the whole, they defined the function of a custom or institution as its contribution to the existence or maintenance of the society as an integrated entity.

---

[35] For reviews of the concept of function, see Firth (1955) and Bateson (1958, Chapter 3); and for an important discussion of the pitfalls of emphasis on function to the exclusion of other considerations, see Dahrendorf (1958).

In both Malinowski's and Radcliffe-Brown's usages, function has to do with how customs and institutions relate to some larger system of interconnected parts, although each usage stresses a different aspect of what we may call the overall ecology of customs. Both usages are alike in emphasizing the effect of customs and institutions on the survival requirements of associated systems—human psychobiological systems in Malinowski's case, and social-behavioral systems in the case of Radcliffe-Brown.

Because of the way in which perceived effects feed back on the structuring of wants and on the definition of purposes, it is tempting at times to assume that an understanding of a custom's effects (its function) also provides an explanation of the custom's reason for being and therefore of its historical cause or origin. But things are not that simple. In our discussion of the development of customs here, therefore, we have not emphasized the actual effects of customs on people and society, but have emphasized the purposes or intended effects for which customs are employed. In this, we have been unconcerned with the nature of these purposes or intended effects. Whether they involved the preservation or destruction of life and society has not mattered to us, for people have customary recipes for committing suicide, when that is what they want to do, as well as for treating sickness, satisfying hunger, and socializing children. For this reason, up to now we have avoided speaking of function, following Linton (1936, p. 404) in distinguishing a custom's "use" from its function.

We have observed that what evolves as a customary recipe or institutional arrangement is likely to have been shaped with reference to a number of different interests and purposes (uses) at once. Some of them are purposes of which the participants are conscious and that they readily admit to themselves. Other purposes and interests may be such that people do not admit they have them, even to themselves. For example, people seem to be unconscious of the emotional concerns attracting them to games, especially when people are devotees or "addicts" of particular kinds of games (Roberts and Sutton-Smith, 1962; Sutton-Smith, Roberts, and Kozelka, 1963). The same is true of much ritual behavior (Whiting and Child, 1953; E. Goodenough, 1965; W. Goodenough, 1966, 1974; Spiro, 1967).

The entire range of purposes and interests whose service people associate, consciously or unconsciously, with a customary practice gives it a positive meaning or value for them. (We speak of meaning here in its connational or associational sense.) At the same time the interests and concerns that are not served and that are even sacrificed give the customary practice a negative meaning or value. Thus meaning and value have both positive and negative valences. People are often ambivalent about their customs. Meaning and value, then, have to do with the way people feel customs relate to them personally—to their wants and concerns, whatever they may be, including their wants and concerns about society as a whole. As changing circumstances alter people's experience of the effects on them of their customs, the meanings and values of these customs will also change. It is in this respect that effects feed back into definitions of purpose and into evaluations of customary means, resulting in rearrangements of what are primary and secondary customs and in the elevation of new recipes to customary status. To this extent a custom's functions (in either Malinowski's or Radcliffe-Brown's sense of the term) can be regarded as helping to explain its existence as a custom, but only to this extent (Spiro, 1966).

It is, of course, very difficult to analyze customs with reference to the purposes people seek to implement by their use and with reference to the satisfactions and frustrations people associate with them and which give them their meaning and value. Interpretations of customary practices that seek to do this, such as psychoanalytically oriented interpretations of religious symbols and rites, are often unconvincing. One of the most important challenges facing the behavioral and social sciences is to devise methods for making such interpretations convincingly. That interpretations involving human motives and purposes are difficult and beset with pitfalls does not allow us, however, to disregard the crucial role of human purpose in cultural theory.

The practice of a customary recipe is, of course, likely to have effects of which people are totally unaware. Such effects can have implications for the satisfaction of basic needs and for the capacity of a society to survive as such. But if people are unaware of them, these effects have nothing to do with the custom's value or meaning for them, nor do these effects feed back into people's changing definitions of purpose and changing evaluations of their customs. In the United States, for example, we have been processing wood pulp in order to make paper and meet other socially approved objectives. At the same time we have been polluting our rivers, something that is not the intended result of this industrial activity. Until recently we were unaware of the extent of the polluting effects, and we undoubtedly continue to remain unaware of the true nature of these effects in all of their ecological ramifications. But these effects are a part of how our wood pulp industry actually functions.

If we think of a customary activity as part of an intricate natural process involving people, their wants, their other activities, and the total environment, then the activity's relation to the process and to all the things involved in it, as understood by an omniscient observer, is its **function**. From the standpoint of its participants, however, a custom has value or meaning, consisting of the ways they associate it with their wants and concerns and with their total life situation (including the state of their environment) as they perceive it. A custom's function thus includes its meaning and value. It includes much more, also. But only its meaning and value are relevant for explaining why a given recipe continues to be a custom or why a given organization of things is maintained as an institution.[36]

---

[36] See the discussion of function and meaning by W. Goodenough (1963, Chapters 4-6) and Linton (1936, Chapter 23). See also the discussion of "manifest" and "latent" function by Merton (1957, Chapter 1). The study of function and meaning and of how function feeds back over time on meaning is, obviously, a matter of major interest in the developing field of "cultural ecology" (Netting, 1971, 1977; Spooner, 1973; Anderson, 1973).

Chapter 6

CULTURE, INDIVIDUAL, AND SOCIETY

We now confront the problems posed at the beginning of this essay:
What is the relation of culture to society?

With language we saw that the individual members of a social group
or community have varying degrees of competence in varying numbers
of dialects and/or languages. They also have understandings among
themselves—common expectations—as to what one of these languages
and dialects in their individual repertories is most appropriate to use
in a given situation. Because it is easier to develop competence in one
than in several different languages, one language in the repertory tends
to become and remain the conventionally established language for
use in all or almost all situations or activities involving the community's
members. This we identify as that community's local language. At the
same time, because each person, through learning, must develop for
himself his own understanding of the content and structure of that
language, no two individuals have exactly the same understanding of
it in all respects. The result is a set of idiolects whose variance from
one another is sufficiently small as to provide a tightly clustered mode.
For the collectivity of speakers, this mode may be considered their
dialect or language. Similar considerations apply to other aspects of
culture. Our discussion of them begins with the individual.

CULTURE AND THE INDIVIDUAL

Out of his own experience each individual develops his private, subjective view of the world and of its contents—his personal outlook. It embraces both his cognitive and his affective orderings of his experience. For technical purposes we shall call it his **propriospect**.[37] Included in a person's propriospect and, indeed, largely dominating its content are the various standards for perceiving, evaluating, believing, and doing that he attributes to other persons as a result of his experience of their actions and admonitions. By attributing standards to others, he makes sense of their behavior and is able to predict it to a significant degree. By using what he believes to be their standards for him as a guide for his own behavior, he makes himself intelligible to them and can thereby influence their behavior—well enough, at least, to permit him to accomplish many of his purposes through them.

A person is likely to find, of course, that the standards he learns to attribute to his parents can for practical purposes also be attributed to at least some others with whom he has dealings, but not to all others. Other persons become sorted into sets or categories of others, each set appearing to have some standards that are peculiar to its membership. By our definition of culture, the standards that a person thus attributes to a particular set of others are for him the culture of that set.[38] That set is for him a significant entity in his human environment regardless of whether or not its members also perceive themselves as an entity or are organized in any way as a functioning group. Insofar as a person finds he must attribute different standards to different sets of others,

---

[37] From Latin *proprio*, "peculiar to the self," and *spectus*, "view" or "outlook." Greek would give us *idiorama*, but I reject this alternative because of the uses to which *-orama* has already been put in other English neologisms. Wallace (1961, pp. 15-16) has referred to the propriospect, unhappily, as the individual's "mazeway." I have referred to it, even more unhappily, as the individual's "private culture" (1963, p. 260). Wallace, too, equated mazeway with culture, saying (p. 16), "Mazeway is to the individual what *culture* is to the group." Here, we shall reserve the term culture to refer to something that is perceived as the property of a set of others.

[38] This conception of culture obviously resembles what the philosopher G. H. Mead (1934, pp. 152-163) referred to as the "generalized other."

he perceives these sets as having different cultures. In this way, each individual's propriospect comes to include several different cultures that he associates with what for him are significant sets of others. This result may be represented as

$$p = (a + b + c + \cdots) + x,$$

in which an individual's propriospect (p) consists of the several cultures $(a, b, c,$ etc.) he attributes to corresponding sets of others, together with such other forms, beliefs, values, and recipes (x) as he has developed from his experience of things apart from other people and that he attributes to no other person.

A person may not only attribute different systems of standards to different sets of others, he may also be competent in more than one of them—be competent, that is, in more than one culture. This is frequently the case among educated Americans of foreign parentage or among people who have gained acceptance in a higher social class than that in which they were raised as children. In the conduct of his affairs a person must choose from the several cultures in his repertory the one he regards as most suitable for his purposes on any given occasion. The one he chooses is his **operating culture** for the occasion. To the extent that he identifies himself with a particular group of others, he regards the culture he associates with that group as *his* culture. We must stress, however, that just as individuals can be multilingual they can also be multicultural, the particular culture that is to be regarded as *theirs*—as when we talk of a person's culture—being determined by considerations of social identification rather than simply of competence (although obviously the culture of the group with which a person identifies himself is very likely to be one in which he is highly competent).

It is worth digressing for a moment to observe that the anthropological concept of culture is itself a product of the common human experience that standards and expectations we learn to attribute to one person can be generalized for practical purposes to some but not to all others. This experience requires people to distinguish different kinds of persons, each kind having to be understood in terms of characteristics and "laws" peculiar to it. If all persons operated in terms of the same standards, presenting no contrasts, the idea of culture would never have been conceived. An anthropologist's account of a people's culture is a statement of the generalizations about standards that he has abstracted from his experience of what is for him a significant set of others and that he attributes to that set as the standards by which its members conduct their affairs.

When individual A perceives individual B to be competent in the standards (the culture) he attributes to group X, and when B perceives A to be competent in the standards he attributes to the same group X, then A and B see themselves and each other as both knowing how to act in accordance with the "same" standards. As they make similar perceptions about other adult members of the group, while at the same time perceiving the contrasting incompetence of children and strangers, they naturally see these standards in which they appear similarly competent as a property of the group itself. As such, these standards appear to exist apart from individuals, who come and go in the cycle of births and deaths. Perceived as the property of a group, as having an independent existence of their own, these standards easily become reified as an object, as something to which people make reference and to which they find themselves responding. As others make demands on us in the name of this object—in the name of what they understand the group's standards to be—we see our own behavior as being constrained, shaped, and even "determined" by it. Thus the standards we project upon the group become a thing to be reckoned with, an external force of major importance for understanding our behavior. From this perspective it is clear why anthropologists as diverse in their views as A. L. Kroeber and Leslie White have agreed in conceiving of culture as supra-individual and as governed by factors other than those governing individual behavior (Kroeber, 1948b). Although this conception is a product of a common human illusion arising from generalizations about others, nevertheless men live by their illusions— by their abstractions and generalizations—and in doing so they make them real.

Strictly speaking, a person's membership in a culture-sharing group is determined by the extent to which he reveals himself as competent in the standards we attribute to other members of the group—by the extent, that is, to which he appears to be enculturated in what we perceive to be the culture of the group. From this viewpoint, it is possible for someone to belong to more than one culture-sharing group, for he can be competent in more than one set of standards. Membership as a matter of cultural competence, we have said, is different from membership in the social-psychological sense of identifying oneself, or being identified and accepted by others, as a member of a group. One may be competent in French culture without having the social identity "Frenchman." Because competence in the standards one associates with a set of others can be developed only through intensive interaction with at least some of those others, the sets of persons who are competent in what they perceive as the same culture overlap very largely the sets of persons who repeatedly participate with one another in one or more activities. The greater the variety of activities in which they repeatedly have dealings with one another, the wider the range of subject matter for which people will perceive themselves as competent in the same standards.

We should stress at this point that a high degree of competence, especially in social behavior and in knowledge of social obligations, can be obtained indirectly by becoming competent in complementary social roles rather than directly by playing the roles themselves. For example, a child develops a great deal of competence in how to act like a father or mother through his interactions with his parents; consequently, when he becomes a parent, what he has perviously learned to expect from his own parents now gives him a clear idea of what to expect of himself. More direct rehearsal of adult roles takes place in play and in games (Roberts and Sutton-Smith, 1962).

Perception of shared competence provides a basis for people to identify one another mutually as being the same kind of persons. It promotes a sense of common ethnicity. It leads people to seek one another out in the conduct of still other activities and gives rise to relatively closed social networks and discrete groups. Whenever we encounter such a social network or group, we assume that in some respects, at least, its adult members can be considered competent in what they perceive to be a common set of standards. We also assume that the standards we learn to attribute to the particular members of a network or group with whom we happen to have dealings are standards that can be safely attributed to the other members of the group and hence to the group as a whole. These assumptions may not always be valid, but the probabilities are in their favor. We operate on the basis of these assumptions until further experience requires us to modify them. Anthropologists have done so in their ethnographic researches just as laymen have done in the conduct of their affairs; they are becoming increasingly aware of the pitfalls of overgeneralizing from the small communities they select for intensive study to the larger ethnic category or "tribe" of which the small community is seen to be a part (e.g., the study by Caughey, 1977).

CULTURE AND SOCIETY

We have mentioned how, when people perceive one another as competent in what they regard as the same culture, this perception reinforces their sense of being a group and their consciousness of kind. But we have not yet attempted a formal definition of the terms "group" and "society."

If we take an activity or some set of activities as a point of reference and examine the frequency with which people deal with one another in connection with it, we shall find that people sort themselves into clusters, those within any one cluster dealing with one another more frequently than they deal with individuals in other clusters, at least in the context of that activity or set of activities. Such clusters are natural groups. If the members of a cluster are conscious of themselves as a continuing entity and distinguish between members and non-members by some criterion of membership (or of eligibility for membership), the cluster constitutes a society in the broadest and simplest sense. This is the sense in which we have been speaking of society here.

There are various classifications of groups and societies according to the kind of activities with which they are associated and according to the manner in which they replenish their memberships, but such classifications do not concern us in this essay. What does concern us is that, in practice, anthropologists have rarely considered simple clusters associated with one or only a few activities as the units with which to associate the phenomenon of culture.[39] Rather, they have looked at all the activities in which people actively engage or on whose performance by others they depend, and have taken as their model of society the cluster of clusters that encompasses all, or nearly all, of these activities and that at the same time appears to form a natural isolate. (For various definitions of society, see Mayhew, 1968.)

These larger, relatively self-sufficient societies may be sharply or vaguely bounded. (For a discussion of boundaries, see Barth, 1969.) Within them, the several subsidiary clusters associated with one kind of activity may be congruent or nearly congruent with the clusters associated with other activities. Household groups within a village, for example, may engage in many different kinds of activities as discrete units. On the other hand, a self-sufficient society's subsidiary groups may differ in composition from activity to activity, overlapping and cutting across one another in membership, as in modern urban populations. Every member of a society may deal with every other member directly, the whole being tightly knit in its interaction patterns; or the members may not all know one another personally, the society being loosely knit and similar to a ramifying network in the way its members deal with one another.

Such differences in group and societal structure are significant for questions relating to the maintenance of social consensus about the content of culture. But it would be unprofitable to try to define the phenomenon of culture with respect to some one kind of group, such

---

[39]To be sure, there have been anthropological studies of hospitals and occupational groups—even of families (Roberts, 1951)—as culture-bearing units. But these groups have been looked at as communities or part communities engaging in a variety of activities, and their study has been infrequent by comparison with studies of village, band, and neighborhood communities. Culture has been so strongly associated with social groups and communities—as distinct from activities—in anthropological practice that one often reads about people as being "members of a culture," a truly nonsensical idea, as is immediately evident if we follow out its implication and speak of people as "members of a language." One cannot be a member of a set of standards or of a body of knowledge and customs. But such are the absurdities to which the equation of culture with group can lead.

as a small, geographically bounded, tightly knit, inbreeding, village community—the kind of community anthropologists have found it easiest to describe. To define culture in such terms is to focus on a special case at the expense of seeing both the phenomenon of culture and its relation to self-sufficient societies in all their complexity, such complexity as we saw illustrated by the case of the Amazonian Indians with which we opened this essay. The relation of culture to such societies is what we now go on to consider.

Obviously, it is to the advantage of people who deal with one another continually for all of them to be competent in what they perceive to be the same standards. Such people arrive at mutual understandings, therefore, as to what standards they will expect one another to be competent in and what standards they will expect one another to use as their operating culture in the activities in which they have mutual dealings. The standards they agree on for this purpose may be said to constitute their **public culture** for those activities.

As we have said, however, people who use what they regard as the same culture in their dealings with one another have each their individual understandings or versions of what that culture is. In their mutual dealings, misunderstandings lead each individually to adjust his own version of the public culture to accord better with the expectations of his fellows. Such adjustments are not made equally by everyone, of course. Some members of the group are acknowledged as more competent than others, and older persons are in general more experienced than younger ones. Consequently, the versions of the group's public culture held by recognized authorities provide the expectations toward which others progressively adjust their own versions. This process of selective adjustment leads to a modal clustering of the individual versions of what all attribute to the group as its public culture.

Objectively viewed, then, a group's public culture is not unlike a biological species, for a species consists of a series of individuals such that no two of them are identical and yet the variance among all of them is contained within limits through the process we call natural selection. The species is thus a modal clustering of physical and behavioral characteristics. Any individual whose characteristics permit him to breed with his fellows is a biologically productive specimen of

the species. The species as a whole can be thought of as a range of
variance or as a set of modal tendencies. But to describe it in terms
of some particular set of characteristics is to make an abstraction
from the objective reality. Individual specimens can approximate this
abstraction but none of them can fully conform to it.

Similarly, a group's public culture consists of the individual versions
of it held by those adult members of the group who are recognized by
other adult members as competent in meeting their expectations of one
another. No two versions are identical as to forms, beliefs, etc., yet the
variance among them is held within limits by the process of selective
adjustment just described—let us call it **normative selection**. Each version (including an ethnographer's) is a socially productive specimen of
the public culture if the person operating with it is adjudged socially
competent by his fellows. We can think of the public culture as com-
promising the range of variance among its socially productive specimens, or we may think of it as a modal tendency among them. But to
describe it is to make an abstraction—an ethnographer's version—which,
at best, can be another socially productive specimen but to which no
other specimen can be expected exactly to conform.

Subjectively, then, a group's public culture consists of the standards
a person attributes to the other members of the group or to the group
as a whole. Thus seen, it is a unitary thing. Objectively, however, a
group's public culture is a taxonomic category comprising the various
subjective versions of the group's public culture held individually by
the group's members. The category contrasts as such with comparable
categories associated with other groups.

Both the subjective and objective views play necessary and important
parts in cultural description and theory. It is important to be clear on
the difference between them and on how each relates to the other. For
example, Hammel (1970) found that 100 Yugoslav informants in
Belgrade gave him 100 different prestige ratings of the same list of
occupations. Two different statistical procedures gave him two different "consensus models" of occupational prestige. One was based
on the entire list of occupations; the other was based on those portions
of the list that were closest to each informant's own occupation, the
"consensus models" for each portion then being put together to make
up an overall model. Each individual had his subjective view of a public

culture relating to occupational prestige, but the ethnographer had to abstract a synthesis of the individual versions to characterize the public culture from an "objective" view.

We have defined a group's public culture as the standards the group's members expect one another to operate with in their mutual dealings. As such, a public culture—viewed either subjectively or objectively— need not contain only one culture in the sense of an organized *system* of standards. Suppose, for example, that we are members of a family in which English is spoken under most circumstances, but French is always spoken at dinner, where English is disallowed. Here members of the same group operate with one another according to two distinct sets of standards for speaking. The public culture I attribute to this family and that I must use as my operating culture to function acceptably as a member of it includes both English and French. This example may strike us as strange, but the phenomenon it illustrates is in fact a common one. Think, for instance, of a school community where football is played in the autumn and baseball is played in the spring, and where all young people are expected to take part in both sports. Two games, so distinct that knowing one is little help in learning the other, are among the things a member of that community must learn in order to operate acceptably in it. Here we would not hesitate to say that football and baseball are both parts of the culture we must attribute to the community. By the same token, the very different bodies of knowledge associated with fishing and with farming, both engaged in by the same men in a village community in Truk, are part of that community's culture.

We have been equating language and culture up to this point, treating both as organized systems of standards for behavior. But in this sense, fishing and farming are two distinct cultures in Truk, just as French and English are different languages. It is clear that when we speak of a society's culture as the things one must know in order to conduct oneself acceptably as a member of that society, we are referring to a number of distinct systems of standards, not just one. These different systems are themselves organized according to higher-level standards or principles that govern what particular system is appropriate to which occasions.

In the examples given, the two languages and the two subsistence activities respectively serve essentially the same kinds of purposes, communicative in the one instance and nutritional in the other. They are thus largely competitive with respect to the purposes they serve and are fitted into the same larger cultural system by being allocated to complementary occasions. Other distinct systems of standards, however, may be complementary as to purpose. Such, for example, would be two systems of standards, one governing activities that serve economic ends and the other governing activities that serve the psychological or spiritual ends we call religious. It is clear that the several major systems of standards in a society's public culture stand to one another in the same kinds of relationship we have already considered in connection with the organization of customary recipes and routines. Thus the same individuals in the United States can profess and practice the ethics of Christianity, of *laissez-faire* business enterprise, and of power politics, each in its own segregated context, without feeling that they are being inconsistent.

In addition to the several systems of standards in a society's public culture in which all of its members are competent there are others in which only some members are competent. Some of these systems may be associated with subgroups within the society, such as organized craft guilds, priesthoods, and the like. Here complementarity pertains to groups and to categories of persons within the society rather than to occasions and purposes alone. Such subgroups or categories may serve as specialists, employing the system of standards in which they are competent to provide services for others. The particular systems of standards so employed are **specialties** within the society's overall public culture. Those in which everyone is expected to be competent, including the standards governing specialist-client relationships, are **universals** in the public culture. (For discussion of cultural specialties and universals, see Linton, 1936, Chapter 16.)

Other systems of standards associated with a specific subgroup may be used by its members regularly when they deal only with one another, as when they use a different language or argot among themselves but not with other members of the larger society. Thus one culture may serve as the public culture of a subgroup while another culture serves as the public culture of the larger society of which the subgroup is a part.

Activities whose performance is confined to subgroups within the larger society are likely to be governed by standards that show considerable variance from subgroup to subgroup. The differences in the several public cultures governing any one of these activities may be noticeable but of a kind that does not seriously interfere with the ability of members of different subgroups to interact on the relatively rare occasions when they must work together in that activity. For such an activity, the degree of difference among the several public cultures of the society's subgroups is analogous to that among dialects of a language. Anthropologists refer to this level of difference as subcultural and speak of the groups as having different **subcultures**. The implication is that culture is to subculture as language is to dialect and species is to subspecies. Here, again, we are speaking of a society's public culture objectively in a taxonomic sense, referring not to a system of standards but to a set of functionally equivalent systems (such as systems of etiquette or agriculture) whose respective contents are such that the behavior of a person operating in terms of one system is not incomprehensible to someone interpreting it in terms of another system within the set. How Christmas is celebrated by Christians in the United States provides a commonplace example of such subcultural differences at the family level. From family to family we find distinct variations in how it is done. The differences are not so great that we are unable to visit back and forth and share our celebration across family lines; but they are there nonetheless.

Associated with specialties and subcultures within a society's public culture are differences among individuals in the extent of their competence. Because competence in a system of standards ordinarily can be acquired only through interaction with persons who are already competent, differences in competence tend to be associated with social boundaries within the larger society. Such differences, therefore, often serve as indications of social identity, such as one's age, sex, caste, or class. Moreover, a person's several competences, among other things, are likely to be his passports to acceptance within the labor gang, professional society, religious congregation, or social club.

Some systems of standards in which individual members of a society may be competent have been learned by them as a result of intimate contact with members of other societies. These individuals do not ordinarily use these standards as part of their operating culture when they deal with members of their own society. They confine their use to dealings with members of the alien societies with which they associate them. But these other systems of standards in their propriospects remain as alternatives in their personal cultural repertories, alternatives to which resort can be made under extraordinary circumstances (compare Linton, 1936, p. 273). They are a part of the society's **culture pool**, in the same way that the languages known to any of a society's members are a part of its language pool, but they have no established role to play in the conduct of any activities involving only members of the society or subgroups within it. They have no place in the society's overall system of mutually ordered public cultures.

This overall system is, of course, what anthropologists usually have in mind when they speak of "a society's culture." It represents precisely the extent of what one has to know, or profess to believe, in order to operate in a manner acceptable to its members in every role that they accept for any one of themselves. As such, a society's culture is not to be confused with the total contents of its culture pool. It is that part of the pool that has acquired customary status for the members of the society or of one of its subgroups. It consists of relatively discrete systems of standards relating to different kinds of activity, the kinds of systems that we ordinarily speak of as language, religion, property, architecture, metallurgy, agriculture, and so on. Every such system, being learned and transmitted independently or semi-independently of every other, constitutes a distinct **tradition**. A society's culture includes not only those traditions that are known to all of its members and that function as universals in its overall public culture, it also includes the traditions that serve as public cultures for only some subgroups within it, either as specialties or as group-specific cultures or subcultures. A society's Culture (let us write it hereafter with a capital C) is, thus, a complex organization of disparate traditions and their constituent parts.

The complicated relationship of culture and society that we have been considering has by now led us to distinguish several senses of the term "culture." Every sense is useful for cultural and social theory, and every one of them is systematically related to every other. We conclude this section by reviewing them as follows:

1.   Culture in the general sense of systems of standards for perceiving, believing, evaluating, and acting. We deal with this sense of the term when we consider the content of culture and its relationship to man's biological, psychological, and behavioral constitution, and when we speak of culture as a pan-human attribute.

2.   The culture of a group, seen subjectively as the system or systems of standards a person attributes to a set of other persons. A person's propriospect may contain several such cultures. We deal with this sense of the term when we consider specific cultures as products of human learning and when we try to describe specific cultures in ethnography, such descriptions being products of ethnographers' learning.

3.   A person's operating culture, being the particular system of standards in his propriospect that he uses to interpret the behavior of others or to guide his own behavior on a given occasion. We deal with this sense of the term when we try to understand the role of culture in social interaction and the processes by which people can be said to come to share a culture.

4.   A group's public culture, being all the individual versions of the system or systems of standards that a group's members expect one another to use as their operating cultures in the various activities in which they have mutual dealings. Each individual's own version of the public culture corresponds to the second sense of the term culture given above. Viewed objectively, a public culture is a category or class consisting of all the individual versions of it, the variance among these versions being contained within limits by the process we have called normative selection. A public culture may consist of several discrete systems of standards, each forming a distinct tradition within it. This sense of

the term culture becomes relevant when we consider culture as the property of a social group and when we become concerned with the maintenance of traditions over time in association with groups.

5. Culture as a particular level in a taxonomic hierarchy of public cultures. It consists of a set of public cultures that are functionally equivalent and mutually apprehensible. Each public culture in the set is a subculture, culture now standing to subculture as language stands to dialect. So employed, the term culture, along with subculture, pertains to the classification of groups according to degrees of similarity and difference in their respective public cultures (or specific traditions within them).

6. A society's Culture (with a capital C), being the overall system of mutually ordered public cultures pertaining to all activities within the society. Here we are concerned with culture as it relates to the organization of human societies in all their complexity.

7. A society's culture pool, being the sum of the contents of all of the propriospects of all of the society's members, including every system of standards of which any member happens to have knowledge. This sense of the term pertains to culture as a reservoir of resources in knowledge and skills carried by the membership of a society. It is especially relevant for understanding the processes of change in a society's Culture (sense 6 above).

THE CULTURE POOL AND CULTURE CHANGE

We have distinguished between a society's Culture (with a capital C) and its culture pool. Its culture pool consists of all the ideas, beliefs, values, recipes, and traditions that are known to one or more members of the society—in other words, everything in every one of its members' propriospects. Its Culture consists of that part of its culture pool that forms a system of traditions functioning as a set of public cultures for the society's members. Figure 1 schematically represents the culture pool of a society, including its Culture with its several component traditions.

---

1. $p_1 = (A_1 : a_1, b_1, -, d_1, -, \dots) \quad + (K_1, -, -, \dots) + x_1$
2. $p_2 = (A_2 : a_2, b_2, c_2, -, -, \dots) \quad + (-, -, -, \dots) + x_2$
3. $p_3 = (A_3 : a_3, b_3, c_3, -, -, \dots) \quad + (-, L_3, -, \dots) + x_3$
4. $p_4 = (A_4 : a_4, b_4, -, d_4, e_4, \dots) + (K_4, L_4, -, \dots) + x_4$
5. $p_5 = (A_5 : a_5, b_5, -, d_5, -, \dots) \quad + (-, -, M_5, \dots) + x_5$
6. $p_6 = (A_6 : a_6, b_6, c_6, -, -, \dots) \quad + (-, -, -, \dots) + x_6$
7. $p_7 = (A_7 : a_7, b_7, -, d_7, -, \dots) \quad + (K_7, -, -, \dots) + x_7$
8. $p_8 = (A_8 : a_8, b_8, c_8, -, e_8, \dots) \quad + (K_8, -, -, \dots) + x_8$
9. $p_9 = (A_9 : a_9, b_9, -, -, -, \dots) \quad + (-, -, -, \dots) + x_9$

. . . .

$n.$ $p_n = (A_n : a_n, b_n, \dots \dots \dots \dots) + (\dots \dots \dots \dots) + x_n$

Figure 1. *Model of a society's culture pool.* The numbers 1, 2, etc. represent individuals in a society with Culture A. After each number is a representation of the contents of that individual's propriospect (p). Within the first parentheses is the individual's version of Culture A and of the various traditions within Culture A of which he has knowledge (a, b, c, d, e). Within the second parentheses are the individual's versions of the Cultures of other societies (K, L, M) with which he happens to be familiar. It would be more accurate, if space permitted, to break down Cultures K, L, and M into their component traditions $(K_a, K_b, K_c,$ etc.). The letter x represents whatever there may be in the individual's propriospect gained from private experience apart from other people and which he attributes to no other persons.

As here illustrated, the society's members are represented by numbers. Each individual has his own version of his society's Culture (represented by the letter A) and its several traditions (represented by the small letters a, b, c, d, and e). Individual 1 is competent in traditions a, b, and d; individual 2 is competent in traditions a, b, and c; and so on. The letters K, L, and M represent the Cultures of other societies in which some individuals in the society of Culture A happen also to have some competence. Thus the propriospect of individual 1 (p_1) indicates a working conception of Culture K (or some traditions within it) as well as an understanding of traditions a, b, and d in Culture A and his private views and understandings (x_1) that he attributes to no other persons.

Every member of the society is competent in traditions *a* and *b* of Culture *A* (let these be such traditions as the language, the norms or rules governing social interaction, the canons of dress). These traditions are cultural universals in the society. Nearly everyone is competent in traditions *c* or *d*, but no one is competent in both (as is usually the case with activities engaged in by only one or the other sex). Only a few individuals are competent in tradition *e*, which is a restricted specialty. Individuals differ as to the number of traditions in which they are competent. Individual 9 is most limited in the range of his competence, while individual 4 is competent in more traditions of Culture *A* than anyone else, except individual 8, and is also competent in two foreign cultures as well. He is clearly potentially an important culture-resource person in his society.

If we concentrate our attention on the column of tradition *a* in Fig. 1, we can visualize several things about it. First, the variance among the individual versions $(a_1, a_2, \ldots, a_n)$ may be such that all individuals see one another as operating with the same tradition. This will be the case if the variance in their individual versions is unimodal in its distribution or is attributed to differences in competence rather than to differences in socially recognized styles or subcultures. The variance may, however, be bimodal or even multimodal, as when different groups within the society have their own subcultural versions of what all still perceive as the "same" tradition. As both rates and kinds of interaction among individuals and groups within the society change, the degree of individual variance and of subcultural difference will tend to increase or decrease accordingly.

As the members of each new generation mature, they look increasingly to one another and less to their elders for confirmation of their competence. Through time, therefore, the modality around which individual variance clusters will itself tend to shift, changing considerably over the centuries without anyone being aware that change is occurring. Such change has been called **cultural drift** (Eggan, 1941, p. 13), in keeping with the already established expression "linguistic drift" for the same phenomenon in language (Sapir, 1921, pp. 165ff.). Cultural and linguistic drift are clearly not to be equated with the biological concept of genetic drift. The latter refers to the loss of alleles from the gene pool of a small population, or to changes in the frequency with which they are represented in such a gene pool, by virtue of chance or random factors as distinct from selective pressures from the environment. The cultural equivalent is loss of a tradition or variant form of a tradition from the culture pool of a small population because the few individuals who are competent in it happen to die before having a chance to pass on their knowledge. As noted by Sapir, on the other hand, the given structure of a language as an organized system of standards and the necessity for a language to continue as an organized system, even while changing, impose important selective pressures that limit the ways in which it can readily change and still remain functionally viable as a language. Thus, selective rather than random processes are at work in linguistic drift. Sapir called attention to striking parallels in phonological changes that occurred independently in English and German over several centuries to illustrate how the phonological structure of a common parent language limits the possibilities for phonological change in its daughter languages.

If members of the society illustrated in Fig. 1 become separated into two societies, the low rate or total absence of interaction between members of the now different groups will permit culture drift to take place independently in each of them and to follow gradually diverging courses. Tradition *a* in each daughter society will eventually become two different traditions (as will other traditions derived from the parent society's Culture). These now different traditions will be "genetically" related, however, in the sense that both have been derived in unbroken, teaching-learning chains from what people in the past had perceived to be the same tradition shared by members of a single society.[40] Depending on the time depths and degree of differentiation involved, such related traditions theoretically can be ordered into genetic categories analogous to linguistic families, stocks, and phyla or to biological genera, families, and orders. But as things now stand, a rigorous comparative method by which to establish genetic relationships in the absence of recorded history—one comparable to that

---

[40]Such related traditions, especially in geographically contiguous areas, are commonly referred to as "co-traditions" in American archaeology (Rouse, 1954, 1957).

developed by linguists—has yet to be created for most aspects of culture. Anthropologists have given much attention to tracing out the origin and spread (technically called "diffusion") of particular traditions (or sets of presumably related traditions) in human history; but so far, our understanding of the nature of culture and of cultural processes has not been sufficient to solve the methodological problems in identifying cognate traditions, a situation that poses a major challenge to future ingenuity and research.[41] To be stressed here is that genetic relationship in culture applies more readily to discrete traditions than to the several articulated traditions that together form a society's Culture.

The process of cultural drift is alone sufficient to produce change in a society's Culture in the course of time, but clearly other processes within its culture pool affect its content. Whereas culture drift is change without discontinuity of tradition, other processes result in change with clear discontinuity of some kind. We can illustrate with reference once more to Fig. 1.

Let us suppose that tradition *e*, the one in which only individuals 4 and 8 are competent, is a body of lore for diagnosing and curing illness and that individuals 4 and 8 are the society's curers. If they should both die without having passed on their knowledge of *e*, this tradition will drop out of the culture pool and will no longer be available to any of the society's members when they are ill.

Obviously, such cultural loss is more likely when there are few individuals competent in a particular tradition. It is also more likely as circumstances reduce the motivation of people to acquire competence in it. Ordinarily there is high motivation to learn those traditions in the culture pools that function as public cultures for the society's members and that are recognized as parts of the societal Culture. And ordinarily there is little motivation to learn traditions in alien cultures from the few local individuals who happen to be competent in them. Under

---

[41] Anthropologists of the German-Austrian school of *Kulturkreislehre*, especially Graebner (1911), addressed themselves to these methodological problems (see the reviews by Kluckhohn, 1936, and by Heine-Geldern, 1964). In the United States, a notable contribution was by Sapir (1916).

ordinary circumstances, therefore, we would expect individual 5's knowledge of traditions in the alien Culture *M* to drop out of the society's culture pool with his death, unless some other individual should have occasion to go live in the society with which Culture *M* is associated and independently become competent in its traditions.

Suppose, however, that individual 5's competence in Culture *M* includes knowledge of a tradition for diagnosing and curing illness different from tradition *e*. The demise of individuals 4 and 8 without having passed on knowledge of *e* will likely create a demand for individual 5 to practice the alien medical tradition he has learned. Thus what was an alien tradition in the culture pool may gain recognition as a public tradition and become a part of societal Culture *A*. Individual 5 may find customers even while individuals 4 and 8 are living, and then *e* and the introduced tradition from Culture *M* will become competing traditions within Culture *A*. Such competition can resolve itself in several ways: one tradition may ultimately displace the other entirely; both may continue, one as preferred, the other as back-up alternative; or they may come to be seen as appropriate to different conditions and become complementary rather than competing.

As the foregoing implies, people's evaluations of what they see as their own and as alien traditions change. Through their inventions and private discoveries, people are continually adding to the *x* component of the culture pool (Barnett, 1953). From contacts with members of other societies they are also continually feeding new elements into the culture pool. These additions may consist of isolated concepts, propositions, value attitudes, skills, or recipes; or they may consist of whole systems of standards, entire traditions. These additions provide referents for reevaluating the ideas, beliefs, recipes, skills, and traditions already established in the societal Culture. Such reevaluations may strengthen commitment to existing principles for conducting the business of life, or they may weaken such commitment. Thus the role, if any, that an element within the culture pool plays in the conduct of activities—as well as its chance of continuing as a part of the pool—is liable to change, as the society's members make different choices among such elements as ways of thinking and acting that seem suitable for accomplishing their purposes and gratifying their wants. Such changes occur at every level of cultural organization, from the substitution of one element for another within a recipe to the substitution of one complete recipe for another, on to the substitution of an entire tradition for another.

Minor substitutions can often be made on an individual basis, as when a farmer decides to try a new crop. But when the expectations of others and, especially, their rights are affected by a substitution, a crisis is likely to develop in the relations people have with one another. When a change in the rules of the public culture is involved, a decision with which all will be expected to comply must be reached, whether by some orderly procedure in the public culture for achieving it or as an outcome of social conflict and the use of coercive force. Other things being equal, such decisions are easier to reach in small groups, such as families, than in large ones. They are easier to reach when commitment to group membership is high than when commitment to group membership is low. Easy or difficult, such decisions are being made continually in all kinds of groups, large and small. Thus in A.D. 1000, Iceland's *Althing* (national assembly) voted to adopt Christianity as the religious tradition with which all Icelanders would operate publicly from then on. Such substitution of one religious tradition for another at the level of public culture has occurred in many other times and places, sometimes with strife and sometimes without it. Different cosmologies, different political orders, different technologies, and different social etiquettes are continually being selected, likewise, from among the alternatives within culture pools to replace old ones (or to coexist with old ones in some ordered relationship) as parts of societal Cultures.

Cultural borrowing necessarily requires that people learn alien cultural traditions, at least in part, usually after they have already become competent in their native cultural traditions. All the possible outcomes that go with second-language learning are also possible in such second-culture learning. An outcome that corresponds to pidginization and creolization of languages is not infrequent. A good example of this last process has been provided by the spread of Christianity as a religious tradition.

When missionaries present Christianity to people they judge to be "primitive," they present it in a form that is stripped down to barest essentials of creed and ritual, hoping that, as time goes on, they can increase their converts' sophistication. The converts learn to follow the ritual forms of a church service or mass; but they tend to invest these forms with meanings that carry over from their own native religious traditions. If the converts are soon left to carry out their newly acquired religious tradition by themselves, with little monitoring by the missionaries, what is likely to result is a local form of Christianity that differs considerably from the parent form, one that incorporates a number of thinly disguised features of the pre-Christian religion and that uses the Christian ritual forms to express religious values and concerns that were expressed by pre-Christian forms.

A good example of such an outcome is displayed by the Catholicism of Maya Indian communities in Guatemala, as revealed in the description of religious practices and concerns in one such community by Reina (1966). What has happened here should not be confused with the kind of syncretism in which alien forms are incorporated in an ongoing native tradition. The Maya consider themselves to belong to the Roman Catholic Church and to be practitioners of a form of Roman Catholicism. Christianity, not the pre-Christian Mayan religion, is the tradition of reference, the one the Maya undertook to learn and to practice as their public, community-wide religion. Their Christianity bears the same kind of relationship to the Catholicism of modern Spain that Haitian Creole bears to modern standard French.

To review in detail the various processes by which changes in public culture are accomplished and the conditions that trigger them and govern the forms they take is beyond the scope of this book. We should note, however, that they often involve emotionally charged, visionary, reform movements that are "utopian" in conception and "totalitarian" in scope.[42] Whatever they involve, the model of a culture pool, as presented in highly simplified form in Fig. 1, provides a frame of reference for examining the processes of cultural change and evolution and for considering the roles of ecology, demography, existing institutional structures, and human psychology and biology in these processes.

---

[42]See the analyses of such movements and their different interpretations by Linton (1943), Wallace (1956), Worsely (1957), Burridge (1969), and Gerlach and Hine (1970). See also Hopper (1950) and Turner and Killian (1957, pp. 307-529).

For it seems clear that when we speak of the cultural evolution of societies, whether they are simple or complex, we speak of the processes governing the content of culture pools and governing the selective use people make of the contents of their own society's culture pool. All of the relevant considerations, whatever they are, are necessarily funneled in their effects through the decisions people make individually and collectively. The influence of environmental circumstances on their decisions is necessarily affected by what people want, unconsciously as well as consciously, for themselves and for their society; and both their circumstances and their wants are mediated by the limitations of their individual propriospects, which include the several cultures, traditions, recipes, and so on, of which they have personal knowledge, and which represent what they have individually made of their previous experiences. The intended and unintended effects of their decisions on the future content of the culture pool, on the environment, and on the structure of institutions—insofar as people are aware of these effects—feed back upon their definitions of purposes in the future and on their perceptions of the choices then available for implementing those purposes.

With this we conclude our discussion of culture, language, and society. We began with questions raised by the linguistic and cultural pluralism of an Indian society in the Northwest Amazon. Taking the familiar phenomenon of language as our point of departure, we then tried to present a way of looking at culture and society that allows us to see their existence as a consequence of how human beings operate as purpose-oriented individuals.[43] Insofar as we have been able to do this, we have also found it possible not only to clarify complexities in the relationship of society and culture but also to delineate a conceptual model that may have utility for a general theory of cultural stability and change.

---

[43]Similar approaches are evident in the writings of Bailey (1969), Barth (1966), Homans (1967), Tanner (1970), and Wallace (1961). Homans states unequivocally (p. 106) that "the central problem of the social sciences remains that posed, in his own language and in his own age, by Hobbes: How does the behavior of individuals create the characteristics of groups?" See also the similar approach to language by Weinreich, Labov, and Herzog (1968).

REFERENCES

Anderson, J. N. (1973). "Ecological Anthropology and Anthropological Ecology." In J. J. Honigmann, editor, *Handbook of Social and Cultural Anthropology.* Chicago: Rand McNally. Pp. 179-239.

Bailey, F. G. (1969). *Stratagems and Spoils.* New York: Schocken Books.

Barnett, Homer G. (1953). *Innovation.* New York: McGraw-Hill.

Barth, F. (1966). *Models of Social Organization.* London: Royal Anthropological Institute, Occasional Paper 23.

Barth, F., editor (1969). *Ethnic Groups and Boundaries.* Boston: Little, Brown.

Bateson, G. (1958). *Naven,* 2nd ed. Stanford: Stanford University Press.

Bauman, R., and J. Scherzer, editors (1974). *Explorations in the Ethnography of Speaking.* London: Cambridge University Press.

Benedict, R. (1934). *Patterns of Culture.* Boston: Houghton Mifflin.

Berlin, B., D. E. Breedlove, and P. H. Raven (1968). "Covert Categories and Folk Taxonomies." *American Anthropologist* 70: 290-299.

Berlin, B., D. E. Breedlove, and P. H. Raven (1974). *Principles of Tzeltal Plant Classification.* New York: Academic Press.

Berlin, B. and P. Kay (1969). *Basic Color Terms.* Berkeley: University of California Press.

Berne, E. (1964). *Games People Play.* New York: Grove Press.

Bickerton, D. (1975). *Dynamics of a Creole System.* Cambridge: Cambridge University Press.

Birdwhistell, R. L. (1953). *Introduction to Kinesics.* Louisville, Ky.: University of Louisville Press.

Birdwhistell, R. L. (1970). *Kinesics and Context.* Philadelphia: University of Pennsylvania Press.

Black, M. B. (1973). "Belief Systems." In J. J. Honigmann, editor, *Handbook of Social and Cultural Anthropology.* Chicago: Rand McNally. Pp. 509-577.

Brown, R., and U. Bellugi (1964). "Three Processes in the Child's Acquisition of Syntax." In E. H. Lenneberg, editor, *New Directions in the Study of Language.* Cambridge, Mass.: M.I.T. Press. Pp. 131-161.

Buchler, I. R., and H. A. Selby (1968). *Kinship and Social Organization.* New York: Macmillan.

Burling, R. (1970). *Man's Many Voices.* New York: Holt, Rinehart, and Winston.

Burridge, K. (1969). *New Heaven, New Earth.* New York: Schocken Books.

Bynon, T. (1977). *Historical Linguistics*. London: Cambridge University Press.

Caughey, J. L. (1977). *Fáánakkar: Cultural Values in a Micronesian Society*. University of Pennsylvania Publications in Anthropology, No. 2. Philadelphia: Department of Anthropology, University of Pennsylvania.

Chomsky, N. (1957). *Syntactic Structures*. Janua Linguarum, Series Minor, No. 4. The Hague: Mouton.

Chomsky, N. (1959). *"Verbal Behavior* by B. F. Skinner." *Language* 35: 26-58.

Chomsky, N. (1965). *Aspects of the Theory of Syntax*. Cambridge, Mass.: M.I.T. Press.

Chomsky, N., and M. Halle (1968). *The Sound Pattern of English*. New York: Harper and Row.

Conklin, H. C. (1955). "Hanunóo Color Categories." *Southwestern Journal of Anthropology* 11: 339-344.

Coon, C. S. (1962). *The Story of Man*, 2nd ed. New York: Knopf.

Dahrendorf, R. (1958). "Out of Utopia." *American Journal of Sociology* 64: 115-127.

Dyen, I. (1949). "On the History of the Trukese Vowels." *Language* 25: 420-436.

Eggan, F. (1941). "Some Aspects of Culture Change in the Northern Philippines." *American Anthropologist* 43: 11-18.

Ervin, S. M. (1964). "Imitation and Structural Change in Children's Language." In E. H. Lenneberg, editor, *New Directions in the Study of Language*. Cambridge, Mass.: M.I.T. Press. Pp. 163-189.

Ferguson, C. A. (1959). "Diglossia." *Word* 15: 325-340.

Ferguson, C. A. (1966). "Assumptions about Nasals: A Sample Study in Phonological Universals." In J. H. Greenberg, editor, *Universals of Language,* 2nd ed. Cambridge, Mass.: M.I.T. Press. Pp. 53-60.

Festinger, L. (1957). *A Theory of Cognitive Dissonance.* Evanston, Ill.: Row, Peterson.

Firth, R. (1955). "Function." In W. L. Thomas, Jr., editor, *Yearbook of Anthropology 1955.* New York: Wenner-Gren Foundation for Anthropological Research. Pp. 237-258.

Frake, C. O. (1964). "A Structural Description of Subanun 'Religious Behavior'." In W. H. Goodenough, editor, *Explorations in Cultural Anthropology.* New York: McGraw-Hill. Pp. 111-129.

Geertz, C. (1973). *The Interpretation of Cultures.* New York: Basic Books.

Gerlach, L. P., and V. H. Hine (1970). *People, Power, Change.* Indianapolis: Bobbs-Merrill.

Girschner, M. (1913). "Die Karolineninsel Namoluk und ihre Bewohner." *Baessler-Archiv* 2: 123-215.

Gleason, H. A., Jr. (1961). *An Introduction to Descriptive Linguistics.* New York: Holt, Rinehart, and Winston.

Goodenough, E. R. (1965). *The Psychology of Religious Experiences.* New York: Basic Books.

Goodenough, W. H. (1963). *Cooperation in Change.* New York: Russell Sage Foundation.

Goodenough, W. H. (1965). "Rethinking 'Status' and 'Role'." In M. Banton, editor, *The Relevance of Models for Social Anthropology.* London: Tavistock. Pp. 1-14.

Goodenough, W. H. (1966). "Human Purpose in Life." *Zygon* 1: 217-229.

Goodenough, W. H. (1967). "Right and Wrong in Human Evolution." *Zygon* 2: 59-76.

Goodenough, W. H. (1970). *Description and Comparison in Cultural Anthropology.* Chicago: Aldine.

Goodenough, W. H. (1974). "Toward an Anthropologically Useful Definition of Religion." In A. E. Eister, editor, *Changing Perspectives in the Scientific Study of Religion.* New York: John Wiley & Sons. Pp. 165-184.

Graebner, F. (1911). *Methode der Ethnologie.* Heidelberg: Carl Winter.

Greenberg, J. H. (1957). *Essays in Linguistics.* Viking Fund Publications in Anthropology No. 24. New York: Wenner-Gren Foundation for Anthropological Research.

Gumperz, J. J. (1962). "Types of Linguistic Communities." *Anthropological Linguistics* 4(1): 28-40.

Gumperz, J. J. (1969). "Communication in Multilingual Communities." In S. A. Tyler, editor, *Cognitive Anthropology.* New York: Holt, Rinehart, and Winston. Pp. 435-449.

Gumperz, J. J., and R. Wilson (1971). "Convergence and Creolization." In D. Hymes, editor, *Pidginization and Creolization of Languages.* Cambridge: Cambridge University Press.

Hall, E. T. (1959). *The Silent Language.* Garden City, N.Y.: Doubleday.

Hall, R. A., Jr. (1965). *Pidgin and Creole Languages.* Ithaca: Cornell University Press.

Hammel, E. A., editor (1965). *Formal Semantic Analysis.* Special Publication, *American Anthropologist* 67(5), Part 2.

Hammel, E. A. (1970). "The Ethnographer's Dilemma: Alternative Models of Occupational Prestige in Belgrade." *Man* 5(n.s.): 652-670.

Harris, M. (1964). *The Nature of Cultural Things*. New York: Random House.

Harris, M. (1968). *The Rise of Anthropological Theory*. New York: Thomas Y. Crowell.

Heine-Geldern, R. (1964). "One Hundred Years of Ethnological Theory in German-Speaking Countries: Some Milestones." *Current Anthropology* 5: 407-418.

Hockett, C. F. (1955). "A Manual of Phonology." Memoir 11 of *International Journal of American Linguistics* 21(1), Part 1.

Hockett, C. F. (1958). *A Course in Modern Linguistics*. New York: Macmillan.

Hockett, C. F. (1966). "The Problem of Universals in Languages." In J. H. Greenberg, editor, *Universals of Language,* 2nd ed. Cambridge, Mass.: M.I.T. Press. Pp. 1-29.

Hoenigswald, H. M. (1960). *Language Change and Linguistic Reconstruction*. Chicago: University of Chicago Press.

Hohfeld, W. (1919). *Fundamental Legal Concepts*. New Haven: Yale University Press.

Homans, G. C. (1967). *The Nature of Social Science*. New York: Harcourt Brace Jovanovich and World.

Honigmann, J. J. (1976). *The Development of Anthropological Ideas*. Homewood, Ill.: The Dorsey Press.

Hopper, R. D. (1950). "The Revolutionary Process." *Social Forces* 28: 270-279.

Householder, F. W., and S. Saporta, editors. (1962). *Problems in Lexicography.* Bloomington: Indiana Research Center in Anthropology, Folklore and Linguistics. Publication 21.

Hunn, E. S. (1977). *Tzeltal Folk Zoology.* New York: Academic Press.

Hyman, H. H. (1968). "Reference Groups." In *International Encyclopedia of the Social Sciences*, Vol. 13. New York: Macmillan and Free Press. Pp. 353-361.

Hymes, D. H. (1961). "The Functions of Speech: An Evolutionary Approach." In F. C. Gruber, editor, *Anthropology and Education.* Philadelphia: University of Pennsylvania Press. Pp. 55-83.

Hymes, D. H. (1962). "The Ethnography of Speaking." In T. Gladwin and W. C. Sturtevant, editors, *Anthropology and Human Behavior.* Washington, D.C.: Anthropological Society of Washington. Pp. 13-53.

Hymes, D. H., editor (1971). *Pidginization and Creolization of Languages.* London: Syndics of the Cambridge University Press.

Hymes, D. H. (1974). *Foundations in Sociolinguistics: An Ethnographic Approach.* Philadelphia: University of Pennsylvania Press.

Keesing, R. M. (1970a). "Kwaio Fosterage." *American Anthropologist* 72: 991-1019.

Keesing, R. M. (1970b). "Toward a Model of Role Analysis." In R. Naroll and R. Cohen, editors, *A Handbook of Method in Cultural Anthropology.* New York: Natural History Press. Pp. 423-453.

Kendall, W. (1968). "Social Contract." In *International Encyclopedia of the Social Sciences*, vol. 14. New York: Macmillan and Free Press. Pp. 376-381.

Kluckhohn, C. (1936). "Some Reflections on the Method and Theory of the Kulturkreislehre." *American Anthropologist* 38: 157-196.

Kluckhohn, C. (1951). "Values and Value-Orientations in the Theory of Action." In T. Parsons and E. A. Shils, editors, *Toward a Theory of Action*. Cambridge, Mass.: Harvard University Press. Pp. 388-433.

Kopytoff, I. (1971). "Ancestors as Elders." *Africa* 41: 129-142.

Kroeber, A. L. (1948a). *Anthropology*, rev. ed. New York: Harcourt, Brace.

Kroeber, A. L. (1948b). "White's View of Culture." *American Anthropologist* 50: 405-414.

Kroeber, A. L., and C. Kluckhohn (1952). "Culture: A Critical Review of Concepts and Definitions." *Papers of the Peabody Museum of Archaeology and Ethnology* 47(1).

Labov, W. (1972). *Sociolinguistic Patterns*. Philadelphia: University of Pennsylvania Press.

Leach, G. (1974). *Semantics*. Baltimore: Penguin Books.

Lehmann, W. P. (1973). *Historical Linguistics*, 2nd ed. New York: Holt, Rinehart, and Winston.

Levine, R. (1973). *Culture, Behavior, and Personality*. Chicago: Aldine.

Lincoln, P. (1975). Parallels in Structure of Lexicon and Syntax Between New Hebridges Bislama and the South Santo Language Spoken at Tangoa. Paper presented at the International Conference on Pidgins and Creoles, January 1975, Honolulu.

Linton, R. (1936). *The Study of Man*. New York: Appleton-Century-Crofts.

Linton, R. (1943). "Nativistic Movements." *American Anthropologist* 45: 230-240.

Malinowski, B. (1925). "Magic, Science, and Religion." In J. Needham, editor, *Science, Religion, and Reality.* New York: Macmillan. Pp. 19-84. (Reprinted in *Magic, Science, and Religion and Other Essays.* Garden City, N.Y.: Doubleday, 1954.)

Malinowski, B. (1944). *A Scientific Theory of Culture and Other Essays.* Chapel Hill: University of North Carolina Press.

Mayhew, L. H. (1968). "Society." In *International Encyclopedia of the Social Sciences,* vol. 14, New York: Macmillan and Free Press. Pp. 577-586.

Mayr, E. (1963). *Animal Species and Evolution.* Cambridge, Mass.: Harvard University Press.

Mead, G. H. (1934). *Mind, Self and Society.* Chicago: University of Chicago Press.

Meigs, A. (1977). *Sexual Ideology and Pollution Among the Hua of Papua New Guinea.* Ph.D. Dissertation, University of Pennsylvania. Ann Arbor, Mich.: University Microfilm Libraries.

Merton, R. K. (1957). *Social Theory and Social Structure,* rev. ed. New York: Free Press.

Metzger, D., and G. E. Williams (1963). "A Formal Ethnographic Analysis of Tenejapa Ladino Weddings." *American Anthropologist* 65: 1076-1101.

Morgan, L. H. (1878). *Ancient Society.* New York: Holt, Rinehart, and Winston.

Mühlhäusler, P. (1974). *Pidginization and Simplification of Language.* Pacific Linguistics Monograph Series B, No. 26. Canberra: Research School of Pacific Studies, Australian National University.

Murphy, J. J. (1954). *The Book of Pidgin English.* 4th ed. Brisbane, Australia: W. R. Smith & Paterson.

Netting, R. M. (1971). *The Ecological Approach in Cultural Study.* Addison-Wesley Module in Anthropology No. 6. Reading, Mass.: The Addison-Wesley Publishing Co.

Netting, R. M. (1977). *Cultural Ecology.* Menlo Park, Calif.: The Benjamin/Cummings Publishing Co., Inc.

Opler, M. E. (1945). "Themes as Dynamic Forces in Culture." *American Journal of Sociology* 51: 198-206.

Parsons, T. (1951). *The Social System.* New York: The Free Press.

Palmer, F. (1971). *Grammar.* Baltimore: Pelican Books.

Palmer, L. R. (1978). *Descriptive and Comparative Linguistics: A Critical Introduction.* London: Faber & Faber.

Paul. B. D., editor (1955). *Health, Culture, and Community.* New York: Russell Sage Foundation.

Pike, K. L. (1943). *Phonetics.* Ann Arbor: University of Michigan Press.

Pike, K. L. (1954). *Language in Relation to a Unified Theory of the Structure of Human Behavior,* Part I. Summer Institute of Linguistics. (2nd rev. ed. The Hague: Mouton, 1967.)

Radcliffe-Brown, A. R. (1935). "On the Concept of Function in Social Science." *American Anthropologist* 37: 394-402.

Reina, R. E. (1966). *The Law of the Saints.* Indianapolis: Bobbs-Merrill.

Roberts, J. M. (1951). "Three Navaho Households." *Papers of the Peabody Museum of Archaeology and Ethnology* 40(3).

Roberts, J. M., and B. Sutton-Smith (1962). "Child Training and Game Involvement." *Ethnology* 1:166-185.

Romney, A. K., and R. G. D'Andrade, editors (1964). *Transcultural Studies in Cognition.* Special publication, *American Anthropologist* 66(3), Part 2.

Rouse, I. (1954). "On the Use of the Concept of Area Co-Tradition." *American Antiquity* 21: 221-225.

Rouse, I. (1957). "Culture Area and Co-Tradition." *Southwestern Journal of Anthropology* 13: 123-133.

Rubin, J. (1962). "Bilingualism in Paraguay." *Anthropological Linguistics* 4(1): 52-58.

Rubin, J. (1973). "Sociolinguistics." In J. J. Honigmann, editor. *Handbook of Social and Cultural Anthropology.* Chicago: Rand McNally. Pp. 479-508.

Sapir, E. (1916). *Time Perspective in Aboriginal American Culture.* Canada Department of Mines, Geological Survey, Memoir 90, Anthropological Series, No. 13. (Reprinted in D. G. Mandelbaum, editor, *Selected Writings of Edward Sapir.* Berkeley: University of California Press, 1949.)

Sapir, E. (1921). *Language.* New York: Harcourt Brace Jovanovich.

Sapir, E. (1927). "The Unconscious Patterning of Behavior in Society." In E. S. Dummer, editor, *The Unconscious: A Symposium.* New York: Knopf. Pp. 114-142.

Sapir, E. (1929). "The Status of Linguistics as a Science." *Language* 5: 207-214.

Schwartz, T. (1962). *The Paliau Movement in the Admiralty Islands, 1946-1954.* Anthropological Papers of the American Museum of Natural History. Vol. 49, part 2. New York.

Sherzer, J. (1970). "Talking Backwards in Cuna: The Sociological Reality of Phonological Descriptions." *Southwestern Journal of Anthropology* 26: 343-353.

Slobin, D. I. (1977). "Language Change in Childhood and in History." In J. MacNamera, editor, *Language, Learning and Thought*. New York: Academic Press. Pp. 185-214.

Smalley, W. A. (1968). *Manual of Articulatory Phonetics*, rev. ed. Hartford: Practical Anthropology.

Sommerstein, A. H. (1977). *Modern Phonology*. London: University Park Press.

Sorenson, A. P., Jr. (1967). "Multilingualism in the Northwest Amazon." *American Anthropologist* 69: 670-684.

Spicer, E. H., editor (1952). *Human Problems in Technological Change*. New York: Russell Sage Foundation.

Spiro, M. E. (1966). "Religion: Problems in Definition and Explanation." In M. Banton, editor, *Anthropological Approaches to the Study of Religion*. London: Tavistock. Pp. 85-126.

Spiro, M. E. (1967). *Burmese Supernaturalism*. Englewood Cliffs, N.J.: Prentice-Hall.

Spooner, B. (1973). *The Cultural Ecology of Pastoral Nomads*. Addison-Wesley Module in Anthropology No. 45. Reading, Mass.: The Addison-Wesley Publishing Co.

Steward, J. H., and L. C. Faron (1959). *Native Peoples of South America*. New York: McGraw-Hill.

Stocking, G. W., Jr. (1966). "Franz Boas and the Culture Concept in Historical Perspective." *American Anthropologist* 68: 867-882.

Sumner, W. G. (1907). *Folkways.* New York: Atheneum.

Sutton-Smith, B., J. M. Roberts, and R. M. Kozelka (1963). "Game Involvement in Adults." *Journal of Social Psychology* 61: 185-199.

Tanner, N. (1970). "Disputing and the Genesis of Legal Principles: Examples from Minangkabau." *Southwestern Journal of Anthropology* 26: 375-401.

Trudgill, P. (1974). *Sociolinguistics: An Introduction.* New York: Penguin Books.

Turner, R. H., and L. M. Killian (1957). *Collective Behavior.* Englewood Cliffs, N.J.: Prentice-Hall.

Turner, V. W. (1967). *The Forest of Symbols.* Ithaca, N.Y.: Cornell University Press.

Turner, V. W. (1969). *The Ritual Process.* Chicago: Aldine.

Tyler, S. A., editor (1969). *Cognitive Anthropology.* New York: Holt, Rinehart, and Winston.

Tylor, E. B. (1903). *Primitive Culture,* 4th ed. John Murray. (First published 1871.)

Valdman, A., editor (1977). *Pidgin and Creole Linguistics.* Bloomington: Indiana University Press.

Voget, F. W. (1975). *A History of Ethnology.* New York: Holt, Rinehart, and Winston.

Wallace, A. F. C. (1956). "Revitalization Movements." *American Anthropologist* 58: 264-281.

Wallace, A. F. C. (1961). *Culture and Personality.* New York: Random House.

Weinreich, U., W. Labov, and M. I. Herzog (1968). "Empirical Foundations for a Theory of Language Change." In *Directions for Historical Linguistics: A Symposium.* Austin: University of Texas Press. Pp. 97-195.

White, L. A. (1949). *The Science of Culture.* New York: Farrar, Straus & Giroux, Inc.

Whiting, J. W. M., and I. L. Child (1953). *Child Training and Personality.* New Haven: Yale University Press.

Witherspoon, G. J. (1971). "Navajo Categories of Objects at Rest." *American Anthropologist* 73: 110-127.

Witkowski, S. R., and C. H. Brown (1977). "An Explanation of Color Nomenclature Universals." *American Anthropologist* 79: 50-57.

Worsely, P. (1957). *The Trumpet Shall Sound.* London: MacGibbon and Kee.